LIVING COLOR

LIVING COLOR

Decorating Your Home with Plants

A. C. Muller-Idzerda & Elisabeth de Lestrieux

in collaboration with
Jonneke Krans

ARCO PUBLISHING, INC.
New York

Published 1981 by Arco Publishing, Inc.
219 Park Avenue South, New York, N.Y. 10003

© Het Spectrum BV 1981

English translation by Marion Jansen

Typeset by ABM Typographics Ltd.,
Hull, England
Printed in the Netherlands
by Royal Smeets Offset BV, Weert

Library of Congress Cataloging in Publication Data

Muller-Idzerda, A.C.
    Living color.

    Translation of: Groener wonen.
    Includes index.
    1. House plants in interior decoration.
I. Lestrieux, Elisabeth de.   II. Krans, Jonneke.
III. Title
SB419.M9613 1981   635.9′65   81-1357
ISBN 0-668-05257-0   AACR2

Contents

Foreword

In our youth we saw the same plants in our home year in year out. This domestic familiarity inevitably bred a certain contempt among youngsters for the traditional array of palms, ferns, clivia, aspidistra and asparagus, but they were simply part of the furniture in every home. No one ever gave a thought to new plants. But if we step inside a flower shop today our eyes are dazzled by the bewildering variety of new foliage and flowering plants on display there. The range is immense; from modest little plants for the narrow windowsill to enormous decorative examples to adorn a hall or the corner of a room. Moreover, nurserymen are now actively responding to the wave of nostalgia that is now expressing itself among the younger generation. Very much as we once switched to the starker, straight lines of cacti and the succulents, after the elaborate romantic taste of our parents, so today's youth are draping their rooms with living curtains and a wealth of evergreen foliage against white walls.

Grandmother's day is also enjoying a popular revival with regard to pot plants: foliage plants again take pride of place, while the more elderly among us still feel the need for a colourful flower here and there. In any event, we would certainly all agree that a house without plants is unthinkable nowadays. As the restrictions of living in highrise city flats or suburban estates with little or no gardens affect our life-style more and more, and we retreat ever further from nature, is it any wonder that the need to surround ourselves with living greenery is becoming increasingly important to us? Not only at home, but also in offices and other places of work. Thus was the term 'office garden' born.

In this book we illustrate and describe the care of new as well as traditional plants, including special methods for growing and combining diverse varieties, with particular attention being paid to their place in your interior design.

Where the plants come from

The keeping of plants is no recent innovation: on the contrary, the techniques and traditions of growing them indoors in pots have been appreciated for centuries. The history of the lotus blossom, cherished by the Pharaohs of Egypt in their palaces 3,000 years ago, gives us the earliest known information on this subject. Also, in the Far East, particularly in ancient China, people were passionately fond of enhancing their homes and formal gardens with flowers and plants.

Originally, of course, each country was familiar only with those plants that flourished in the local environment, but as contacts with other continents and countries increased, people began to discover the possibilities of plants from distant lands. In Europe, during the eleventh and twelfth centuries, many hitherto unknown exotic plants were introduced by Crusaders returning from the Holy Wars. This early import later continued on a larger scale with the expansion of merchant shipping to more remote countries. Explorers and enterprising botanists also brought many new plants back with them, which were promptly added to the cherished collections of an ever-growing number of plant enthusiasts. Every university was proud of the unique plants in its botanical gardens, and as more and more specimens poured into Europe, certain rare varieties became the subject of crazes. In the sixteenth century Holland already boasted its own nurseries, and during the Golden Age merchants from the republic of North Netherland suddenly became obsessed with tulips of mixed colours. So began the famous tulip mania that hit Europe around 1630, with speculators paying incredibly high prices for a single tulip bulb. This boom lasted about a decade and was followed a century later by a similar craze with the hyacinth as the object of trade. The discovery and collecting of plants in all parts of the world came into its own in the second half of the eighteenth century. Botanists and doctors of medicine studied many exotic plant varieties and sought good and efficient means of transporting them back to Europe. *Anthurium, Dieffenbachia, Monstera* and *Philodendron*, for instance, originally came from America, as did many of the bromeliads; and from Japan came, among other worthies, *Primula japonica* and *Thunbergia* (Black-eyed Susan).

A bewildering range of plants is now widely available to everyone, and you can choose at your leisure which plants from this vast collection you find most attractive.

Below respectively: Primula japonica *was brought back from Japan in the last century, and* Protea barbigera (*Sugar Bush*) *which is native to South Africa and Australia.*

Right: The Guzmania *hybrid is a bromelia-type hybrid which has its native habitat in Peru and Columbia. Opposite page:* Cordyline *is found in Asia, Australia and Africa.*

Inexpensive houseplants

Friendship is often best expressed, and sustained, with little gifts. And there are, after all, many occasions when a large plant or elaborate trough would be out of place. Moreover, children sometimes like to buy a small plant with their pocket-money. So it is nice to know that they, too, are well catered for. Most flower shops have a wide choice of small plants suited to the most modest pocket.

The varieties mentioned below are small, cheap and longer lasting than a bunch of flowers.

Begonia semperflorens hybrids. These well-known, long-flowering begonias show masses of small single flowers in a variety of colours in April–May if they are sown from seed in January–February. Tip cuttings can also be rooted in water.

Campanula isophylla 'Alba' (Italian Bellflower or Star of Bethlehem). A very well-known trailing houseplant which produces a wealth of white, star-shaped flowers, ideal for hanging baskets.

Campanula isophylla 'Mayi' (China-blue Bellflower). As well known as 'Alba', with somewhat larger flowers and leaves.

Catharanthus roseus (Madagascar Periwinkle). A low-growing little plant, showing clusters of flat, five-lobed flowers. It has small, oval, dark-green leaves with a light central vein. Flowers March–October. Although a perennial, it is best propagated from stem cuttings.

Coleus (Flame Nettle or Painted Nettle). Grown for its multi-coloured leaves, which are at their best in full light and sun. Insignificant, purple flower spikes should be pinched out as soon as they appear. Tends to run wild if over-wintered, so it is better propagated by rooting stem-tip cuttings in water in spring or late summer.

Chrysanthemum vestitum hybrids (*syn. C. morifolium*). The compact indoor chrysanthemum. Flowers for a remarkably long period in an enormous variety of colours. After flowering it can be planted out in the garden where it will give pleasure for many years as a high, cluster-chrysanthemum.

Echeveria glauca. A succulent with flat rosettes of grey, fleshy leaves with a bluish tinge, and graceful orange–red flower clusters with yellow tips. Flowers between April and June.

Kalanchoe blossfeldiana. A succulent with a wealth of red, white or pink flower umbels rising above spoon-shaped leaves, which is available practically throughout the entire year. Coarser-leaved strains have more colour variations; their flowers are also larger and the stems usually longer.

Pelargonium zonale hybrid. The Dwarf Geranium 'Black Vesuvius', a low-

Below: Impatiens walleriana, *better known as Busy Lizzie. Bottom:* Catharanthus roseus, *also called* Vinca rosea. *Right:* Campanula isophylla '*Alba*', *the Italian Bellflower, can be grown as a hanging plant.*

growing plant with dark purple-brown leaves and single flowers in every shade of orange.

Primula praenitens (syn. *P. sinensis*, Chinese Primrose). Low, rosette-forming growth, long hairy stems with flower umbels in a large variety of colours; velvety, swollen lobed leaves. Flowers in the autumn and winter. Can sometimes be overwintered if flowers are removed as soon as they have finished blooming.

Rhipsalidopsis gaertneri (Easter Cactus). Related to the link-leaf cacti, with rectangular, leaf-like branching stems. Scarlet tubular flowers, which open in a wide star shape, appear on the tips of the plant in spring.

Saintpaulia ionantha (African Violet). A very popular little plant that is available all year round in a variety of tints with single or double blooms in, mainly, clusters of purple, pink, white or blue flowers.

Saxifraga stolonifera (Saxifrage, Mother of Thousands or Strawberry Geranium). The triple-coloured cultivar 'Tricolor' is a particular favourite. The rosette-shaped plants grow young plantlets at the end of trailing thin stems. The mother plant itself, which has dark-green leaves with red undersides, often produces small white flower plumes in the summer.

Far left: The Pelargonium zonale *hybrid 'Friesdorf'. Below left: Low-growing* Chrysanthemum vestitum *hybrid, the so-called Pot Chrysanthemum. Left:* Rhipsalidopsis gaertneri, *a spring-flowering link-leaf cactus. Below: The familiar houseplant* Kalanchoe blossfeldiana.

Houseplants without problems

Some houseplants demand a great deal of attention. They require a specific amount of feeding, moisture and rest at precisely the right time, and consequently not everyone is in a position to cultivate these delicate varieties. Fortunately, there are also plants which will thrive with less careful nursing. The varieties mentioned below can take a knock or two. They often do very well in the homes of people whose busy lives leave them little time for pampering plants; and those of us born without green fingers!

Billbergia nutans (Queen's Tears). An easy-care bromelia, with a rosette of long, sword-shaped leaves that have a curving growth habit. The plant can bloom for months on end with tubular flowers of red, green and yellow. But like every bromelia, it does so only once in a lifetime. However, it does form new offsets at the base and brings them to maturity before it dies off.

Chlorophytum. Commonly known as the Spider Plant because of the spider-like appearance of the young plantlets that grow from the long and trailing flower stems, and sometimes as St Bernard's Lily. The all-green *Chlorophytum capense* is the least demanding, and also needs less light than the other varieties. The cultivar *Chlorophytum comosum* 'Variegatum' with finely striped green and cream leaves is, however, the most popular, but if it is put in too dark a position the fine markings will fade from the leaves.

Cissus. An exceptionally hardy climbing shrub. This applies particularly to

Billbergia x windii, *an easily cultivated bromelia, is a cross between* B. decora *and* B. nutans.

Cissus rhombifolia (*Rhoicissus rhomboidea*), a shrub with red-brown hairy stems and characteristic, diamond-shaped triple compound leaves.

Cyclamen. A well-known corm-plant. The most popular species is *Cyclamen persicum*, with large red, pink or white flowers. There are also many cultivars ranging in colour from white to deep crimson. The richly blooming miniature cyclamens with small flowers are particularly sturdy.

Cyperus alternifolius. Also called the Umbrella Plant. The tiny light-brown flowers grow from the centre of the leaf rosettes which curve outwards like the spines of an umbrella.

Fatshedera. Also known as the Tree Ivy, it is a cross between an ivy and japonica. It has large, glossy leathery, ivy-shaped leaves and often grows to a great height. A support is then indispensable. *Fatshedera lizei* is the best known strain; *Fatshedera lizei* 'Variegata', having leaves with creamy-white margins, is prettier but more difficult to maintain.

Hedera (Ivy). A well-known genus for evergreen climbers of which there are very many species and strains both for indoors and outdoors. The strongest strains include the small-leafed *Hedera helix* 'Chicago' or 'Pittsburgh', whose deeply incised leaves have pointed lobes.

Philodendron scandens (Sweetheart Vine or Lover's Plant). Originally a climber, but also does well as a trailer or in a hanging basket.

Sanseveria. Commonly known as Mother-in-Law's Tongue or Bowstring Hemp. *Sabsevieria trifasciata* has dark-green leaves with feathery transverse markings; the strain 'Laurentii' has yellow bands edging the green leaves.

Tradescantia (Spiderwort). An old-fashioned trailing plant. The strongest variety is the green *Tradescantia albiflora*; a more lively species is the creamy-striped 'Albovittata'. *Tradescantia blossfeldiana* is virtually indestructible, providing it is placed behind a sunny window. Also called the 'Flowering Inch Plant' it has a more creeping growth habit, with leaves covered with soft hairs and tinged with purple on their undersides.

Below respectively: Cyperus alternifolius, *the ever-popular indoor Umbrella Plant.* Tradescantia blossfeldiana, *also called the Flowering Inch Plant, blooms profusely in the summer.*

Left: Fatshedera lizei, *a well-known crossing of Ivy and the False Castor Oil Plant.*

Unusual houseplants

As our modern houses and flats are provided with all manner of comforts such as open-plan interiors, picture windows and thermostatically controlled central heating, it is not surprising that the interest in tropical plants is very much on the increase. Providing sufficient care and attention is paid to their individual needs, these more exotic plants will thrive in the home. You may, however, have to go to a little extra trouble to acquire one or two of the plants mentioned here.

Anthurium andreanum (Oil Cloth Flower, Tail Flower, Painter's Palette). Is the bigger sister of the Flamingo Flower, *Anthurium scherzerianum*. Its large, glossy, leathery spathes have earned this plant the name Oil Cloth Flower. The colours vary from red, orange, salmon and flesh-pink to rose, white and greenish. The plant, with its oblong, heart-shaped leaves, grows fairly tall and is happiest in a temperature of 16–22°C, in a humid atmosphere. Spray generously and often, especially when the heating is on, and keep well watered, preferably with rainwater. Place in a light position but away from direct sunshine. Although it is customarily propagated from seed, the enthusiast will generally propagate by division, planting the young offshoots separately in a proprietary peat compost, preferably mixed with half part sphagnum moss, or a special anthurium soil. Ensure good drainage by placing pieces of broken clay (crocks) at the bottom of the pot.

Callistemon citrinus. Better known as the Bottle Brush Plant because of the cylindrical, brush-like flower spikes, consisting almost entirely of red stamens. This is an evergreen shrub from Australia. The young leaf is covered with a silvery to red hairy down. If the blooms are not removed after flowering, new inflorescences can form.

The Bottle Brush Plant is not very demanding, and even likes to be placed outdoors in the summer. Overwinter in a light, sunny position at 6–10°C. Propagate by stem cuttings, preferably with a heel, in August–September. Likes rather acid soil; there is now a proprietary loam-based compost available for acid-loving plants. Raise both cuttings as well as mature plants at 12–16°C. When they show a sturdy growth, top the cuttings and await flowering, which generally takes place in spring and summer.

Coffea arabica (Arabian Coffee). Known as the Coffee Plant, this is a tall, evergreen shrub bearing leathery, elliptic leaves that look rather waxy along the central vein. The growth habit is remarkably willowy, with vertical and horizontal branches. Compact clusters of aromatic white flowers appear in the leaf axils in September, followed by fruits which turn red when ripe. These are stone fruits which usually contain two stones—the famous coffee-beans, that are flat on the side where they grow against each other. The plant can flower and fruit in the greenhouse but this seldom happens in the home environment. Propagate from seed or lateral stem cuttings with a heel in late summer. It is advisable to add a little loam or clay to the potting compost.

Medinilla magnifica (Rose Grape). A robust, large-leafed shrub, originating in Indonesia, with a beautiful show of wing-like rosy-pink bracts under which hang clusters of dusky-pink anthers, like a bunch of grapes. No easy houseplant, it really needs a warm, humid greenhouse but it is possible to grow this elegant species in the house, provided it is carefully tended, given a light, sunny position and well shaded from the rays of the noonday sun. Flowering usually takes place during spring and summer. Water liberally during growth and feed with a proprietary fertilizer or natural humus every 14 days. Maintain humidity by spraying profusely and often; water less after flowering and maintain at a temperature of 15°C.

Pisonia alba (*Heimerliodendron alba*). From Australia, New Zealand, Hawaii and Tahiti, it greatly resembles *Ficus elastica*. The white and green variegated cultivar 'Variegata' is particularly popular. A robust foliage plant that needs a light position, shaded from the noonday sun, at a temperature of 18–22°C. It will reach a height of 2–4ft and looks good standing alone as well as in mixed company in a trough. Water generously during growth and sponge the leaves It can eventually be treated with a proprietary leaf-gloss every

From top to bottom: Medinilla magnifica, *originating from Indonesia.* Ananas comosum, *the ordinary pineapple as houseplant.* Coffea arabica (*Coffee Plant*) *can be grown in greenhouse and living room.*

three or four weeks. Water more sparingly during the winter and make sure that the pot is not left standing in water. Give it a little houseplant fertilizer now and then but only from March to November. If the plant gets too tall, propagate by stem-tip cutting or air-layering; cuttings should have at least one eye and be planted in sand and peat with a soil temperature of 25°C. Repot in a peat-moss based compost with fine clay or loam.

Rhoeo spathacea (Moses-in-the-Cradle or Boat Lily). Better known by the name *Rhoeo discolor*. Lance-shaped leaves with purple undersides. The cultivar 'Vittatum' is enhanced by having yellow stripes along the upperside of its leaves. The first common name describes its remarkable flowering habit—clusters of little white flowers are borne within large cradle or basket-shaped purple bracts. Emanating from Central America, the *Rhoeo* is related to the well-known *Tradescantia*. Position in a good light away from direct sun. It likes a temperature of 18°C during the winter and not below 12°C at night. Water moderately and maintain a humid atmosphere. If necessary, pot on in spring in a peat-based compost with sharp sand. Propagate from cuttings or seed in February–March.

Scirpus cernuus (Miniature Bulrush). Found all over the world. Grass-like stems and leaves tipped with white, fluffy flower spikes. Grows straight up initially then arches far over the sides of the pot, a habit that makes it highly suitable as a decorative hanging plant. Like its cousin, the Umbrella Plant, it is a real 'water-baby'; if the environment is too dry or it is not watered sufficiently, the tips of the thin leaves will quickly curl under and scorch. Position in a good light out of the sun at a temperature of 12–20°C. Spraying is better than watering, but always ensure that there is water in the saucer or plantpot. If necessary, propagate by division in spring. Leaf-mould mixed with clay or loam makes a good compost, although this plant also thrives in water with a feeding solution (hydroponics).

Callistemon citrinus, *better known as the Bottlebrush Plant. This plant can grow to a height of more than one metre.*

Plants for the shade

Not all plant enthusiasts are fortunate enough to have a sunny window at their disposal. They may find themselves with a room facing north or northeast, where plants can simply fade away through lack of sunlight. Another handicap is that such a sunless room can be very cool in the summer. But not only people in the proverbial bedsitter or limited accommodation have this problem. Those living in large houses where the front or rear faces north or northeast also need to make a careful choice of attractive plants to enhance those parts of the house that are less suitably positioned, or catch little or no sunlight. Fortunately there are plenty of sturdy plants that are quite happy in front of a sunless window or in a cool room. Full light is often more important than sun.

Below are a number of flowering plants that actually prefer shadow.

Calceolaria (Slipperwort). Frequently referred to as Slipper or Purse Flower, it flowers in the spring and is happier in a cool, humid atmosphere than a warm, dry one. This little plant also does well somewhere in the middle of the room.

Camellia japonica (Camellia). Requires a very light situation facing north. An evergreen, it flowers in the spring or in the winter, depending on its position. It is advisable to leave this plant in its original position; do not turn it when the bud is developing or during flowering.

Clivia (Kaffir Lily). Best-known variety is *Clivia miniata*, a plant which is easy to grow and bring into flower. It needs a permanent, light position facing northeast or northwest. Flowers in the early spring and sometimes again in the late summer.

Right: Howeia forsteriana, *the familiar Kentia Palm with long, feathered leaves. Below:* Calceolaria (*Slipperwort*) *requires a light spot out of the sun during the growing and flowering period. Bottom:* Philodendron mamei *is a climbing plant originating from Equador.*

Cyclamen persicum (Cyclamen). Flowers in winter and spring with large pink, red or white flowers. This most popular of pot plants likes light and airy conditions, while the ideal temperature is 10°C.

Primula malacoides (Fairy or Baby Primrose). An annual, with a limited colour range. The flowers grow at different levels and the stems are covered in mealy farina.

Primula obconica. A perennial, of which many strains have been developed in a wide range of colours. The plant flowers practically throughout the entire year.

Apart from the abovementioned flowering plants, there are also a number of foliage plants that can be maintained without sun.

Aspidistra elatior (Cast-Iron Plant). Thrives in a position with little light and even dislikes sunlight!

Chlorophytum (Spider Plant). A plant for a light or moderately light position. The *C. comosum* 'Variegatum' with long, narrow leaves with a white centre stripe, is the species almost exclusively cultivated as a houseplant.

Howeia forsteriana (Kentia Palm). Has elegant leaves divided into four arching leaflets that spread out like a fan. Likes a light to moderately light situation away from sunlight, but with a humid atmosphere.

Monstera deliciosa. Popularly known as the Swiss Cheese Plant, Hurricane Plant or Mexican Bread Fruit. Prefers a light situation, but happily tolerates a place in the shade.

Nephrolepis (Sword Fern or Boston Fern). A plant that is eminently suitable for a rather dark, not too warm room, provided a moist atmosphere prevails.

Polystichum falcatum (Shield Fern). Suitable for a moderately light, cool position. This plant will not tolerate sunlight.

Philodendron (Sweetheart Vine or Lover's Plant). A decorative plant related to the *Monstera*, which requires a humid atmosphere. Tolerates very shady situations.

Rhaphidophora aurea. Better known under the erroneous name *Scindapsus aureus*, it forms aerial roots and yellow-blotched or -streaked, heart-shaped leaves. The cultivar 'Marble Queen' is almost white and slow growing.

Schefflera venulosa. Related to the Ivy and the Castor Oil Plant, this plant needs only moderate light, little or no sun and cannot tolerate draught. Water only when the soil is dry. Temperature: 15–20°C. Sponge the leaves and treat with a leaf-gloss.

Scindapsus pictus (Devil's Ivy). A white-flecked climber which can be attractively cultivated as a hanging plant. The leaf markings will fade if it is deprived of sufficient light. Likes to be kept warm.

Tradescantia albiflora 'Albovittata' (Spiderwort). A hanging plant with a cream-coloured, striped leaf. Can be grown throughout the year in a shady position under a normal living room temperature.

Well-known plants with a moderate growth rate and evergreen foliage are *Dracaena*, *Ficus*, *Pandanus* and *Sansevieria*.

If necessary, these plants will be quite satisfied with poor light and have no particular desire for a place in the sun.

Top to bottom left: Cultivar of Camellia japonica. *A blue* Primula obconica.
Clivia *in bloom.*
Cyclamens *flowering in the spring.*

Houseplants in the summer

There are plants that will thrive in the most shady situations and others that are true sun-worshippers. The first group need a sunless position that allows only the early morning sun to infiltrate a little; for example, facing north or northeast. But even for plants that like standing in the sunshine there is a risk in the fierce heat of the noonday sun—although some species with coloured and hairy leaves are extremely tolerant in this respect. Always protect your plants from the afternoon sun by some sort of screen or blind, should this be too much of a good thing for them.

Like us, plants can also suffer in the summer through lack of fresh air. Open a top window if possible or use a ventilator to allow the rising warm air to escape. If the noise of traffic will permit it, open your windows during the day. Some plants respond very well to being placed outside during the summer, but it is better to 'plunge' the plants complete with their pots in a bed of earth than simply to stand them somewhere outdoors. This can cause the root-ball to dry out, and the plant could also be knocked over by the wind. It is advisable to put your plants outside in good growing weather. However, when they are taken indoors again in the autumn, be careful not to tear any of the roots that may have grown through the bottom of the pot. It helps if you turn the pots in their earth bed every two weeks, lifting them a little at the same time, if possible. This will curb the plant's natural inclination to put out too many roots both in and through the pot, particularly during active growth. When you plunge the plants in the earth, allow some space under the pot to prevent garden pests from entering through the drainage hole.

They can also be placed on a balcony or patio, plunged in suitable tubs or troughs filled with peat fibre. Large plants can also be placed outside in their tub or trough; pack these large containers in black plastic to prevent drying out. Don't put the plants outdoors too early; night frost can be a common occurrence at the beginning of May and this is fatal for all houseplants.

Above: Coleus (*Flame Nettle*) *likes lots of sunlight. Top: The attractive, sun-loving* Beloperone guttata. *Right: Detail of the same plant, also known as the Shrimp Plant.*

Plants need far more moisture in the summer than in the winter, and if plants are watered early in the morning they are better able to tolerate the heat of the day. With some species the soil is already dried out again by evening, and these should be given a second watering. However, it is better for cactus plants to be dry again before evening.

Plants that are placed outside during the summer must be checked daily. Restricted in their pots, they profit little from the moisture and food in the surrounding soil.

Most plants are in full growth during the summer, and in this busy period they not only need more water but also regular feeding. Flowering plants are greatly aided by a weekly feed of houseplant fertiliser and foliage plants respond well to a fortnightly spray with a proprietary foliage feed, which is dissolved in water and sprayed onto the leaves. We can give acid-loving plants, such as bromelias and ferns, an organic fertiliser, or alternate an organic feed with a compound liquid fertiliser.

Summers out of the sun:
Achimenes, Adiantum, Aechmea, Aglaonema, Anthurium, Aphelandra, Asparagus, Asplenium, Begonia rex, Billbergia, Blechnum, Calathea, Chamaedorea, Cissus, Columnea, Fatshedera, Fatsia, Ficus, Fittonia, Hedera, Howeia, Impatiens, Maranta, Microcoelum (Coconut Palm), *Microlepia, Monstera, Neoregelia, Nephrolepis, Nidularium, Odontoglossum, Paphiopedilum, Pellaea, Peperomia, Philodendron, Phlebodium aureum* (syn. *Polypodium aureum*), *Phoenix, Piper, Platycerium, Rhaphidophora aurea* (*Scindapsus aureus*), *Ruellia, Saintpaulia, Scindapsus, Selaginella, Sinningia* (Gloxinia), *Streptocarpus, Vriesea.*

Sun-loving houseplants:
Acalypha, Allamanda, Alternanthera, Begonia semperflorens, Beloperone, Bougainvillea, Caladium, Catharanthus roseus (*Vinca rosea*), *Coleus, Euphorbia milii* (syn. *E. splendens*), *Gynura, Hibiscus rosa-sinensis, Pelargonium zonale* 'Black Vesuvius' and 'Friesdorf' (Dwarf Geraniums), *Setcreasea, Thunbergia, Tradescantia blossfeldiana.*

Houseplants that like to be out in the garden during the summer:
Abutilon, Azalea indica, Camellia, Citrus, Fatshedera, Fatsia, Fuchsia, Grevillea, Hydrangea macrophylla (Hortensia), *Lantana, Nerium oleander, Passiflora, Pelargonium* (Geranium), *Phyllocactus, Sparmannia, Zantedeschia, Zygocactus.*

Top to bottom: Streptocarpus *hybrid, cannot tolerate direct sunlight.* Hibiscus rosa-sinensis *hybrid is a sun-loving plant. While* Ficus benjamina *needs screening from direct sunlight. Left:* Bougainvillea spectabilis *really enjoys sun and light.*

19

Houseplants in the winter

Nowadays, with our centrally-heated houses, it is difficult for us to imagine the struggle houseplants must have had surviving the winter in grandmother's day. Yet although modern homes present greater opportunities for indoor cultivation, we still often make life much more difficult for our houseplants than it need be. There are often very warm and ice-cold rooms in one and the same house. And at night when the heating is turned down, or off, the temperature around the windowsill, where most of air plants stand, drops dramatically. Casually, we simply expect them to get used to it!

From outside to inside

The first problems arise with the transition from outdoors to indoors. Plants that have spent the summer in the garden, or on a balcony or patio, usually find themselves suddenly whisked indoors. As soon as night frost is in the air, they are rushed into the house again, giving them no chance to acclimatise slowly to their new environment. One minute they are in the fresh air and the next on the windowsill of a warm room. It's a wonder they survive this traumatic change! If at all possible, you should first bring them into a sunny but unheated room which can be ventilated daily. Most of the plants returning from their summer sojourn will find it easier to readjust to life indoors at a temperature of 10–15°C. Other norms apply for the so-called greenhouse plants that spend the summer outdoors in tubs or plant-troughs, and because of their limited winter hardiness require a cool but frost-free overwintering; the conservatory or cool greenhouse answered this need in former days. A temperature of 5–8°C is sufficient for *Nerium oleander*, *Agapanthus*, *Agave americana* (mistakenly called the Century Plant Aloe), *Citrus* species, laurels, pomegranates, *Camellia*, *Lantana* and most fuchsias. Delicate and special cultivated varieties feel happier during the winter at 10°C. 'Conservatory plants' generally only need a soil watering once a week. Other plants, that spend their dormant period in a rather warmer environment, must be carefully checked for leaf-fall; this probably means that the atmosphere is too dry. Such is often the case with azaleas. It is therefore recommended that you spray these every other day over the crown until the buds begin to colour.

Frost danger

Overwintering plants must never be watered if the soil still feels moist and is dark in colour. Most cacti, with the exception of the leaf-cacti, can manage entirely without water between November and March at a maximum temperature of 10°C. It is a fact that in a cool environment most plants die from too much rather than too little water. Plants that shed their foliage in the autumn can also overwinter without water, such as *Achimenes*, *Sinningia* (Gloxinia), *Rechsteineria* (*Gesneria*) and *Hippeastrum* (Amaryllis). The

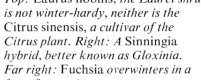

Top: Laurus nobilis, *the Laurel shrub, is not winter-hardy, neither is the* Citrus sinensis, *a cultivar of the* Citrus *plant. Right: A* Sinningia *hybrid, better known as Gloxinia. Far right:* Fuchsia *overwinters in a frost-free environment.*

temperature for these plants must definitely not fall below 6°C, although a higher temperature is better.

Garden geraniums (*Pelargonium : onale*) are often kept in a cellar or attic during the winter. They are usually the first plants to suffer from frost, and in order to prevent frost damage generally, protect your plants with newspaper at night and remember that even in a heated room the air behind the windows can still be icy cold. So never leave plants on a windowsill behind closed curtains! During a period of frost plants standing in an unheated room should not be watered, as a wet root-ball can freeze in no time.

Central heating

Now that many of our houses are equipped with central heating, those of us who were used to open fires or stoves find it difficult to keep our plants healthy. With the innovative district-heating system the temperature is seldom as high as it is with individual heating systems, although nowadays even district-heating can usually be controlled with a private thermostat. But whatever the case may be, radiator heat creates an extremely dry atmosphere. A room thermometer will enable you to check the temperature and a hygrometer will give you the moisture content of the air; these are invaluable aids, especially if you have a large collection of plants. An atmospheric humidity reading of 70 is ideal for most plants, and as soon as the indicator drops below this level, it will be necessary to spray regularly. There are also other measures we can take to help maintain a moisture atmosphere for our plants. We can place them on a small trellis above a drainage trough or tray filled with water, or on a small 'island' of pebbles or moist peat in a tray or shallow trough. Keep the amount of water level with the pebbles but see that your plants do not get 'wet feet'. The evaporating moisture around the plant creates a sort of 'microclimate', and several plants can be grouped together on a large tray or moist peat bed. The drier the atmosphere the more chance there is of shrivelled leaf tips and leaf-fall.

That is why small water containers hung over the radiators, or special humidifiers are generally a 'must' in most homes. In an interior that houses a large number of plants it is well worthwhile investing in an automatic electric humidifier. One heating system that has been gaining ground recently is that of radiator panels installed along the wall, in the ceiling or under grilles in the floor. The gently and evenly circulating warm air actually has a beneficial affect on plants; the principle of this particular system being based on a lower surface temperature and a relatively high atmospheric humidity.

Most tropical plants need a day temperature of 18–22°C during the winter, not dropping below 15°C at night. Hardier plants can suffice with a minimum night temperature of 10–12°C. Winter-flowering houseplants are usually less happy with a high temperature and a somewhat dry atmosphere than foliage plants. Various winter-flowering begonias are quite at home with a temperature of 12–15°C. An *Azalea indica* in bud is even satisfied with 6–10°C. A *Clivia* develops its buds at 8–10°C, and a *Camellia* must definitely not be warmer than 10–16°C. The *Cyclamen*, which is rather difficult to cultivate in a centrally heated room, prefers a temperature of 12–16°C. *Crassula portulacea* and *C. arborescens*, older specimens of which really cheer up a room in winter with their white flower umbels, are satisfied with 6–10°C. *Euphorbia fulgens* and *E. pulcherrima* (Poinsettia, Christmas Star) prefer a little warmth and are happy at 18–20°C. After its resting period, a *Hippeastrum* bulb should receive ground warmth, about 20°C, to promote the emergence of the bud. *Kalanchoe blossfeldiana*, in bud or flower, is satisfied with 12–16°C. Primulas abhor high temperatures and can generally suffice with 12–15°C, while *P. malacoides* even prefers a cool 10°C. The *Zygocactus* (Christmas Cactus) in bud and in flower is content at 16°C.

Below: The natural growing period of the Crassula portulacea *falls in the winter. Bottom:* Azalea indica *flowers both in winter and spring.*

Ferns

Although ferns never bear flowers, they are welcome, evergreen guests in the home, where they thrive best in the shade. Ferns belong to the spore-bearing plants. Lacking flowers, they cannot multiply themselves from seed but do this by giving off spores, which develop on the undersides of the leaves, particularly on older leaves. That is why during the ripening period we can find brown powder on our plants, windowsill and table. Unfortunately, it is virtually impossible to propagate ferns from the spores.

Ferns with fibrous rooted leaves can be propagated from stems to which a small section of the rootstock (rhizome) must be attached.

The species we cultivate in the home are closely related to our indigenous forest ferns but originate in the tropics. In their native tropical rain forest they grow under a dense mantle of trees, as ground cover or as 'epiphytes': living on the branches and trunks of trees, rooted in the remains of rotted wood and foliage. They like shadow and need a moist bed and atmosphere. Because of their tropical origin, ferns are happiest in moist warmth; the most favourable temperature, however, varies according to the species.

The plant likes to stand on an 'island' of water (provided the water level is just below the bottom of the pot) or in an outer container packed with moist peat or moss. But always keep the compost in the pot moist. It is really better to use rainwater or tapwater that has been kept standing in the watering-can for at least 24 hours. And always use tepid water. You can now buy plastic drainage trays or troughs with raised ridges along the bottom, on which the pots can stand without the risk of a soggy 'foot-bath'. Most ferns like a moist, cool spot away from the sun, and whoever gives them a little care will be rewarded with really attractive plants that are not all that demanding and can last for years.

Some indoor fern species and their characteristics

Adiantum cuneatum (Maidenhair Fern). Wiry black stems carry delicate, light-green dentate leaflets. Difficult to keep in the living room because of its sensitivity to draught and a dry atmosphere; more suitable for the bathroom. Shrivelled fronds should be cut off at soil level. The plant puts out new shoots at the base. Raise young plants at 18°C and spray daily.

Asplenium nidus (Bird's Nest Fern). This has large, shiny, leathery leaves that form a deep, nest-shaped rosette at the base of the plant. Has a distinct darker central vein. Temperature: 18–20°C. Brown to black blotches will appear if the temperature drops too low or fluctuates rapidly. Very sensitive to sun. Can only be propagated from spores.

Nephrolepis exaltata (Sword Fern or Boston Fern). Has long, single-feathered, bright green leaves. The cultivars 'Rooseveltii' and 'Whitmannii' are rather more attractive with deeply incised fronds; the latter also has double-feathered, more crinkly fronds.

Pellaea rotundifolia. A low-growing, bushy fern with small, leathery and shiny rounded leaves, and hairy spines and stems. A strong plant for the living room. Temperature: 12–16°C. Guard against direct sunlight.

Phlebodium aureum (syn. *Polypodium aureum*, Hare's Foot Fern). A trailing

Top to below right: Platycerium bifurcatum (*Stags-horn Fern*), Phlebodium aureum, Adiantum scutans roseum (*Maidenhair Fern*), Pteris cretica (*Ribbon Fern*) *and* Nephrolepis exaltata (*Sword Fern*).

fern with long, deeply incised, feathery leaves with an attractive blue-green sheen and crimped edges. The distinctive creeping rootstock of this plant is furry scaled and twines all over the pot. Temperature: 16–20°C.

Platycerium bifurcatum (Stag-horn Fern). An epiphytic fern with two distinct kinds of leaf: the fertile, thus spore-bearing, often hanging, deeply incised antler leaves are initially covered with white downy hair; while the sterile anchor leaves, which are broad and flat, grow upwards from the base, forming a protective shell-like shield, giving the appearance of a plant in a pot. Temperature: 16–20°C. Needs a high degree of humidity and must be protected from draughts and direct sunlight.

Polystichum falcatum (*Cyrtomium falcatum*, Shield Fern). The hardiest of the indoor ferns, with single-feathered leaves that have a shiny, leathery appearance and are deeply incised. Temperature: 8–16°C. Sometimes over-winters successfully in an unheated, frost-free room.

Pteris cretica (Ribbon Fern). A hardy fern with single feathered leaf-fronds. The lowest leaves are also incised. There are clear differences between the sterile and fertile leaves: the latter carry spore clusters on the underside of the leaves, which are narrower and have longer stalks.

An unfurling leaf of Phlebodium aureum.

Palms

Palms are woody plants which in their natural habitat can grow into impressive trees. They belong to the family *Palmae* and are unilobed. As palms are mainly indigenous to tropical and sub-tropical countries, we are becoming steadily more familiar with them through our journeyings to distant and sunny climes. The only European species is the dwarf palm *Chamaerops humilis*. In the tropics and sub-tropics the majority of palms serve an economically vital purpose. Who is not familiar with the date-, coco-, sago-, raffia- and rattan-palm as sources of food, oil and fibres? Palms are divided into feather and fan palms, according to the shape of their leaves; most of our indoor palm plants belong to the first group. The leaves are feathered and grow outwards from a single long, flexible stem. To this group belong, among others, the *Chamaedorea*, *Howeia* (Kentia Palm), *Microcoelum* (Coconut Palm), and *Phoenix* (Date Palm).

The fan palms include, among others, the *Chamaerops* and *Livistona*. Belgium is the primary importer of palm seed, and has professional palm nurseries in the city of Ghent. The seeds (stones) of the Date Palm, even those of the confectionery dates in their paper-lace boxes, can easily be sown and raised by a patient enthusiast. But generally speaking, palms are imported from Belgium and further cultivated for commercial distribution. Palms are intrinsic plants from grandmother's day, both as ornamental houseplants and as the traditional decor at all manner of social functions. One could even hire them from the florists for receptions, weddings, and so on. In those days there was hardly a house without a palm in front of the window, which is probably the reason why the following generation shunned this rather austere house decoration. Now that nostalgia rules the day, the

Microcoelum weddelianum *or Dwarf Coconut Palm, with its graceful pinnate leaves that can reach one metre in length.*

palm has regained its once honoured place, particularly among today's youth, who have taken to foliage plants with a vengeance.

Palms root downwards rather than across, so it is better to use a high, narrow pot or container than a wide, shallow one. For compost we would recommend one part all-purpose loam, one part leafmould or peat moss, and one part dried cow manure. Palms must be repotted as soon as the roots grow through the drainage hole at the bottom of the pot, and in April if possible. They like to be watered liberally in the spring and summer, less in winter. They are also grateful for regular spraying over the leaves and a light shower of summer rain. If we want to keep the leaves shiny and healthy they can eventually be treated with a foliage gloss product every 3 or 4 weeks; for more delicate leaves it is better to use a spray. Feed with plant fertiliser only during the growing period.

Brown tips, the bane of many indoor palms, are often present in the making, so to speak, as the tender young leaves yet unfurled are joined together at the edges, which causes wounds when they tear loose. Too high a temperature or too dry an atmosphere can also easily result in brown tips. If this is the case they can be snipped off, but allow at least 1mm of the leaf to remain or a new wound will occur. Information about the requirements of individual species—temperature, atmosphere, location, care, etc.—can be found in the illustrated houseplant dictionary at the back of the book.

The true Date Palm, Phoenix dactylifera, *that abounds in North Africa.*

Below: A decorative fan palm called Livistona chinensis. *Bottom:* Chamaedorea elegans, *the Dwarf Mountain or Parlour Palm, Mexico.*

25

Climbing and hanging foliage plants

The versatile use of trailing and climbing plants to decorate walls with a subtle curtain of greenery is becoming increasingly popular. However, if you don't want your 'living walls' actually to take over your home it will be necessary to use the pruning knife from time to time! Variegated and coloured foliage plants are less demanding than the flowering species. They really flourish grouped together in a plant-trough, as an attractive frame around doors and windows or trained along a trellis as a cheerful room-divider.

Asparagus densiflorus (syn. *A. sprengeri*, Asparagus Fern). Not a fern, but an ivy—and a typical hanging plant from grandmother's day. The long wiry stalks do not carry leaves but tiny needle-like branches known as phyllo-clades. Hardy plant for a moderate temperature.

Cissus antarctica (Kangeroo Vine). A member of the vine family. It is one of the strongest and more robust growers against a sunless wall. The saw-edged, light-green leaves with their distinct markings resemble the birch leaf.

Cissus rhombifolia (*Rhoicissus rhomboidea*, Grape Ivy). This has triple, diamond-shaped leaves growing at right angles along brown hairy stems. Young shoots are covered with a white hairy down and the leaves have a dark-green, metallic sheen. Is more tolerant of cold and fluctuating temperatures, with 10°C as minimum.

Cissus striata (Miniature Grape Ivy). A dainty, small-leafed species, with five diamond-shaped, bronze-green leaflets radiating from reddish stalks.

Davallia bullata (Rabbit's Foot or Squirrel's Foot Fern). An elegant fern with finely dissected arching fronds and an unusual creeping, grey hairy rootstock which hangs over the edge of the pot, looking rather like a rabbit's foot.

Ficus pumila (*F. repens*, *F. stipulata*, Creeping Fig). A self-clinging species of the climbing ficus, with small, kidney-shaped leaves which stand out at right angles along the stem. Using its ivy-like tendrils, it can cover large areas of wall.

Ficus radicans 'Variegata'. The cream and white variegated leaves are supported by a creeping stem, which develops roots and buds from its runners if laid along the soil.

Right: The sturdy climber Philodendron scandens, *with its heart-shaped, leathery leaves. Below: The* Hedera helix *species* 'Glauca' *is a popular climbing plant. Bottom: The cultivar* Oplismenus hirtellus 'Variegatus' *is a trailing or hanging grass.*

Glecoma hederacea 'Variegata'. Has small, white-flecked leaves and is, according to the name of the species, vine-like, but its leaves are actually kidney-shaped. Occasionally forms small blue flower clusters.

Hedera canariensis 'Variegata' (syn. *H. canariensis* 'Gloire de Marengo', Canary Ivy). The most widely cultivated variegated ivy, with large, light-green leaves with creamy-white markings, that grow widely spaced along the stem. It is a slow grower for a light situation.

Hedera helix 'Crispa'. Has small leaves that have a distinct wavy, crimped appearance and grow densely along the stem.

Hedera helix 'Glacier'. Attractive, small-leafed, variegated ivy with grey-green three-cornered leaf, the edges of which are flecked with silvery white; sometimes also has pink margins. Care: as for *H. canariensis* 'Variegata'.

Hedera helix 'Goldheart'. Small tapering ivy leaves with golden-yellow centre and dark-green edge. Reddish stems. Care: as for *H. canariensis* 'Variegata'.

Hedera helix 'Pittsburgh'. One of the best-known indoor ivy plants, with small, pointed leaves. Forms adhesive aerial roots and is tolerant to changes in temperature.

Below to bottom left: Peperomia pereskiifolia, Rhaphidophora aurea, Ficus pumila, Hedera helix *hybrid and* Cissus antarctica.

Oplismenus hirtellus 'Variegatus' (Basket Grass). Hanging or creeping grass, with long, slender stems and narrow, spear-shaped green leaves with white and pink stripes; looks rather like a *Tradescantia* but for its typical 'grass joints'.

Peperomia glabella 'Variegata'. Has a trailing growth habit; pinky-red stems and shield-shaped, light-green leaves with a creamy margin. Care: as for *Peperomia pereskiifolia*.

Peperomia pereskiifolia. Russet stems carry fleshy, elliptical leaves with distinct parallel veins, arranged in a group of four around the bud. Grows erect initially, then adopts a trailing habit.

Philodendron ilsemannii. A climbing stem carries large, almost white leaves, marbled grey/green. More difficult to cultivate than the green-leafed philodendrons.

Philodendron scandens (Sweetheart Vine). One of the hardiest climbing plants, with heart-shaped, leathery leaves that grow on long stalks straight up the climbing stem. Excellent for north-facing rooms.

Piper nigrum (Black Pepper). A robust hanging plant with egg-shaped, leathery black-green leaves. A slow grower that also does well in less advantageous situations. Care: as for *Peperomia*.

Rhaphidophora aurea (syn. *Pothos aureus*, *Scindapsus aureus*). Comparable to a variegated *Philodendron scandens*. A vigorous climber which tolerates a less suitable location provided the temperature remains above 15°C.

Stenotaphrum secundatum 'Variegatum'. A hanging grass with long stems and striped leaves with a creamy-white margin. Care: as for *Oplismenus*, but raise under a somewhat cooler temperature.

Syngonium vellozianum (syn. *S. auritum*, Goosefoot Plant or Arrowhead Plant). A high-growing climber, related to *Philodendron* with aerial roots and large, three to five-lobed leaves.

Tradescantia blossfeldiana. A creeping plant with boat-shaped, downy, bronze-green leaves with purple undersides. Clusters of small lilac flowers appear from the tips of the stems. This plant is extremely tolerant both of sun and a dry, warm room.

Flowering, climbing and hanging plants

Top: Clerodendrum thomsoniae.
Above: Allamanda. *Below:*
Hypocyrta glabra.

We seldom give it much thought, but most of the climbing and hanging plants we know never flower. There are, of course, flowering species, but we hardly ever see them in plant-troughs or the like, since this is not a congenial place for them. They like plenty of fresh air and sun, while most plant-troughs are usually situated at some distance from an airy window. In addition, flowering plants require individual care, which becomes rather difficult when they are grouped together with others in a container. But the flowering trailers, climbers and hanging plants cover such a large range that, in spite of the extra care they need, they are well worth our attention.

Allamanda. A vigorous climber with oval, rather waxy leaves and large trumpet-shaped, orange-yellow or yellow flowers on the tips of the stems during the summer.

Bougainvillea glabra. Renowned climbing plant with inconspicuous white flowers surrounded by violet bracts that look rather like butterfly wings. Comes into all its glory on a light, sunny porch or balcony where it will grow against the wall and roof.

Campanula isophylla 'Alba' (Italian Bellflower or Star of Bethlehem). The white flowers normally come into bloom from July to September. Although nowadays flowering specimens can be seen on display in florists in autumn and in February–March.

Campanula isophylla 'Mayi' (China-blue Bellflower). Lilac-blue; flowers around August–September but generally less profusely than 'Alba'; is also less vigorous.

Clerodendrum thomsoniae (syn. *Clerodendron*). A twining plant, which loses its foliage during the resting period from October to February. In summer it bears dense clusters of scarlet flowers surrounded by white calyces.

Columnea (American Goldfish Plant). An ideal plant for hanging baskets, with leathery or hairy leaves that grow in pairs opposite each other along the long trailing stem. Bears red, orange-red or orange tubular flowers from the leaf axils in late winter and spring; can also flower in late summer and autumn.

Dipladenia. Bears magnificent trumpet-shaped flowers along its twining stems throughout the summer; the young plant has a bushy growth. The strains *D. sanderi* (salmon-pink) and *D. boliviensis* (white) are favourites.

Fuchsia. The hanging species used to go by their colour, but are now commercially available by name. During the flowering period in spring and

summer they can eventually be cultivated outdoors in a half-shady situation. Indoors they should be given a light, well-ventilated location—if possible in the morning sun.

Hoya carnosa (Wax Plant). A climbing plant with large, oval, leathery leaves and pendant flower umbels in the axil of the leaf. The waxy, white to pale-pink flowers with a bright red centre, are fragrant, particularly at night. Do not remove faded flowers, as new buds will form therefrom. Needs good light but shade from the hottest sunshine.

Hypocyrta glabra. An attractive hanging plant, related to *Columnea*, with small, thick fleshy leaves and little orange-yellow flowers in the leaf axils in winter and early spring.

Manettia bicolor. A twining plant that bears pairs of long, tapering leaves on opposite sides of the stem. Striking little tubular, short-stalked scarlet-with-bright-yellow flowers bloom from the leaf axils during the early summer, autumn or later.

Passiflora caerulea (Blue Passion Flower). A well-known climbing shrub with runners that put out clinging tendrils. Produces dramatic, large blue star-shaped flowers from early summer to autumn.

Pelargonium peltatum (Ivy-Leafed Geranium). A hanging or trailing geranium with smooth, ivy-like leaves and white, pink, crimson or lilac flowers throughout the entire summer. Cultivate in a good light but shade from the midday sun.

Plectranthus oertendahlii (Prostrate Coleus or Swedish Ivy). A trailing plant that has small, velvety, saw-edged leaves with purple undersides on rectangular violet stems. In the autumn bears 2-lipped white or pale lilac flowers, that from a distance look like small lilacs. Needs a light to moderately light location shaded from the afternoon sun.

Plumbago auriculata (syn. *P. capensis*, Cape Leadwort). A climbing shrub with limp stems and clusters of sky-blue, phlox-like flowers that appear from the leaf axils from spring to late autumn, sometimes even to December. The removal of dead blooms prolongs the flowering period.

Stephanotis floribunda (Madagascar Jasmine). The famous bride's bloom. A fragrant, twining shrub with white, star-shaped, waxy flowers in the leaf axils. Normally makes its appearance in the spring and summer but the flowering season can now be lengthened by extra lighting—known as the 'long day treatment'.

Thunbergia alata (Black-eyed Susan). A perennial climbing plant that is nevertheless usually grown as an annual. The flat-petalled cream, yellow or orange-yellow flowers often encircle a dark heart (eye). Flowers from May to June to well into autumn. It looks lovely in a hanging pot on the balcony or climbing up a cane or little trellis on the windowsill.

Top to bottom: Passiflora caerulea (*Blue Passion Flower*), Dipladenia splendens, Thunbergia alata (*Black-eyed Susan*). *Bottom left:* Stephanotis floribunda, *better known as Madagascar Jasmine.*

Cacti and other succulents

Many plant lovers have the idea that cacti and other succulents are 'dull'. But this is not so, for these unique plant groups with their beautiful, often sculptural shapes, fascinating woolly growth and frequent gorgeous colouring, are certainly worthy of our attention. The abstract shapes of some of the columnar species also fit surprisingly well into modern interiors, and the number of enthusiasts and collectors of these intriguing plants has consequently grown considerably in recent years.

Succulents

Although cacti are, in fact, succulents (from the Latin *sucus* = sap), they are generally spoken of separately because there are certain differences between cacti and other succulents that are related to many other plant families. Succulents owe their name to the cell tissue of their roots, stem or leaves, which are adapted to store large amounts of water in adverse conditions. These storage organs consequently become thick and fleshy, thus presenting the smallest transpiring area for a given volume of water. This characteristic, however, is not exclusive, since it is also a feature of a number of species that belong to a non-succulent plant family.

As a matter of fact, many people enjoy the company of succulents without knowing it. The popular, red-flowering *Kalanchoe blossfeldiana*, for instance, is a succulent, as is the *Sansevieria*, with its long, spear-like leaves (yellow-edged in the cultivar *Sansevieria trifasciata* 'Laurentii'), and *Euphorbia milii* (Crown of Thorns), with its sharp spines and clusters of salmon-red flowers. Another subtle succulent much cherished for generations is *Aloe variegata* (Partridge Breast Aloe), so often seen on the windowsills of farmhouses in Holland. Other examples are *Ceropegia woodii* (String of Hearts or Rosary Vine), with its long, slender, trailing stems, little heart-shaped leaves and purple-brown flowers, and *Hoya carnosa* (Wax Plant), an ideal houseplant, with its shining green leaves and beautifully marked waxy flowers. In short, the range of succulents is as varied as it is wide.

The majority of succulents are very fond of sunlight, but there are also species that tolerate shadow. In general, however, they thrive in plenty of light and also some fresh air now and then. Succulents, the *Agave*, for example, can create an interesting and often dramatic effect standing on their own, and so are now being used more often as solitary plants. Give them a spotlight if their location is poorly lit.

Other good 'loners' are the many species and strains of *Euphorbia* (Spurge), tall-growing plants, often with artistic, abstract shapes. The best species of succulent *Euphorbia* are *E. grandicornis*, *E. coerulescens*, *E. lactea*, *E. triangularis* and *E. trigona*. The low-growing *Euphorbia* also make excellent houseplants, as do most species of the *Crassulaceae* (stonecrop family); even when these plants are not in flower, they are still a delight to the eye. They are to be found among the genera *Crassula*, *Dudleya*, *Echeveria*, *Graptopetalum*, *Pachyphytum* and *Sedum*.

Those of us who possess a south-facing windowsill can derive much pleasure from the genera *Aloe*, *Gasteria* and *Haworthia*.

Below to bottom right: Euphorbia trigona, Ceropegia stapeliiformis, Sedum (*a low-growing succulent shrub, not winter-hardy*) *and* Crassula lycopodioides.

Cacti

The cultivation of cacti goes back a very long time. Growers were already collecting cacti in Greek and Roman times, but their endeavours then, as now, were not always an unmitigated success. In fact there is a great deal of misunderstanding about the correct care of these plants, which is rather surprising, as they are really quite easy to cultivate. The majority of cacti require plenty of sun and warmth during their growing season.

Large windows and broad windowsills facing the sun are a good location. Cacti can tolerate high temperatures in the summer providing they receive sufficient water and fresh air during the day. They flourish well in long, fairly roomy pots or troughs made of black plastic or other non-porous material, such as black pewter or glazed china. In containers without drainage holes it is necessary to layer the bottom with pebbles, crocks or gravel, which will absorb any surplus water. Depending on the species, give little or no water in the winter; the ideal temperature at this time is $\pm 10°C$. A cool environment discourages growth, which should not occur in the dormant season, since it is likely to be thin and elongated. Gradually increase watering as the weather gets warmer. The compost in which cacti are bedded should contain a good percentage of drainage material, either sharp sand or horticultural perlite or both. Special cactus compost is now available commercially.

From the large range of cacti, we select for the home those varieties that are particularly remarkable for their strange, sculptural form, handsome spine formation, bizarre hairy growth or spectacular and easy flowering. The small-staying *Opuntia* (Prickly Pear), the weirdly shaped columnar *Cereus* (Peruvian Torch), the colourful, spined and fuzzy-haired *Mammillaria*, and the easy-flowering *Rebutia* (Dwarf Cactus) offer a wide choice for the composition of a decorative, small collection on the windowsill.

Even for less sunnily situated houses one can still choose suitable specimens from the original epiphytic cacti and their various strains. *Epiphyllum* hybrids (orchid cacti) offer a large variety of white, pink, purple and red flowering plants.

Zygocactus truncatus (Christmas Cactus or Crab Cactus) which flowers in winter, is a particularly popular plant. This species can also spend the summer in the garden. The *Aporocactus* (Rat's Tail Cactus) is a beautiful hanging plant that blooms richly with rose-red flowers. The *Rhipsalis* (Easter Cactus or Mistletoe Cactus) is also a good room plant, with small, white or light-yellow flowers in winter.

Top: Opuntia ficus indica (*Fig Cactus*). *Above:* Epiphyllum *hybrid.*

Above left: Mammillaria guelzowiana. *Bottom left:* Zygocactus (*Christmas Cactus*). *Below:* Rebutia (*Dwarf Cactus*).

Home grown herbs

We have recently rediscovered herbs, and thereby acquired a new taste, and nose, for adventure. The fragrance of lavender once more wafts from many a linen cupboard and the aroma of parsley and thyme again permeates the kitchen. Thanks to herbs, many people have again become their own flavour-expert—quite happy to forego the convenience of frozen, dried or canned foods for the pleasure of experimenting with new recipes and ancient herbs.

This revival is apparent in the increasing number of shops now selling herbs in all manner of forms. Dried herbs in bags or pots are now available at every self-respecting grocery store, supermarket and large chemist; you can choose from a reasonable selection of herb plants at markets, while, finally, bags of herb seed with specially prepared pots of soil are now also available.

Fresh herbs from a flowerpot

Thanks to herb seeds and the potted herb plants, it is now possible for every-one—even a city-dweller in a high-rise flat facing north—to cultivate his own little herb garden: in flowerpots on the windowsill. Many have found it a good idea to start off with a clump of chives, with the soil-ball attached, and a second pot of self-sown parsley. If you have a balcony, you can, of course, be a little more ambitious. You will be surprised at the number of delicious and aromatic varieties you can grow in roomy, well-drained pots, provided you protect the plants from draughts and guard against drying out, frost and pest attacks. When space is limited it is better to buy young plants than to raise them from seed yourself. Then you will not get too many plants of one variety taking over, neither will you have to wait too long for results. (Opposite is a summary of some herb varieties that can also be bought as plants.)

Incidentally, many herbs combine well with the profusely flowering summer annuals that brighten our balconies at this time of the year. We are thinking here of rosemary (perennial), marjoram, thyme, chives, sage, lavender, hyssop, mint, borage and the perennial savory. A single plant of any of these is sufficient.

Parsley, celery, chervil and watercress—herbs that give us a rich crop—are best planted afresh a few times or sown in separate boxes or pots.

Top: Savory is an annual herb. Above: Various bunches of herbs hanging up to dry.

Drying your own herbs

The aromas of the various herb varieties are apparently at their strongest in the middle of a sunny day, so this is the best moment to cut your herbs for drying. Most of the plants should be picked just before flowering, and if you don't cut them back too far, the plant will shoot out again and so provide a second crop. The freshly cut herbs should be hung upside down in fairly loose, airy bunches in a dry spot out of the sun. They can also be dried in the oven: slowly in a low heat, quickly in a hot oven, that has, of course, been turned off. In both cases, the oven door should be left slightly ajar and the herbs spread out thinly on a baking tin. They are sufficiently dried when the stems become brittle and snap off crisply. Then rub the leaves from the stalks and store them in airtight jars or tins.

To buy as plants

Southernwood, lemon balm, tarragon, hyssop, mint, lavas, lavender, woodruff, marjoram (perennial), horseradish, peppermint (black-leafed), pimpernel, rosemary, sage, true winter and yellow lemon thyme.

Annual and annually grown herbs

Anise, basil, savory, borage, dill, camomile, chervil, garlic, cummin, coriander, marjoram, parsley, celery, garden cress, thyme (French summer), fennel.

Perennial plants

Absinth, chives, savory, lemon balm, tarragon, hyssop, caraway, mint, lavas, lavender, woodruff, marjoram, horseradish, peppermint, pimpernel, rosemary, sage, thyme (German winter).

Page 32, bottom left: A herb garden can be cultivated on a balcony.
Below: Herbs can be preserved in well-sealed pots, tins or drums.

Indoor orchids

Although there are some wild orchids indigenous to our regions, the great majority grow in tropical climes. It took a long time before the imported tropical plants could be successfully cultivated here, mainly because, initially, so little was known about the growth factors that prevailed in their original environment. The more exacting cultivation requirements of these exotic plants make it rather difficult to get reasonable results if you try to grow them in an ordinary living room, which is generally too dry and too cool. A centrally-heated room with a particularly moist atmosphere offers greater possibilities than one with an open fire or stove. And anyone attempting to grow orchids in a room heated with a gas fire or oil stove is almost certain to be disappointed.

The most congenial environment for orchids is a terrarium, a glass plant case (Wardian), or a specially constructed plant window, fronted with sliding glass panes, in which both temperature and humidity are automatically controlled. But as with all plants, it is a matter of imitating their natural environment as much as we can.

Orchids that can be cultivated in the living room with a reasonable chance of success are, among others, *Coelogyne cristata*, *Odontoglossum grande* (Tiger Orchid), *Odontoglossum pulchellum* and *Paphiopedilum insigne* (Slipper Orchid).

The first three varieties are so-called epiphytic or tree-orchids. They have pseudobulbs and in their natural environment do not grow on the ground but nestle on the trunks or branches of trees. The fourth species is a terrestrial- or earth-orchid: it has no stem or pseudobulb and roots in the soil.

Whether a plant belongs to the orchid family or not is determined not only by its appearance, original habitat and the pattern of the veins on the leaves, but especially by the structure of the flower. Plants with flowers showing great similarity in their composite parts are classified as one family.

The flower of the orchid usually has six petals, or apparently only five where two are united as in Venus' Slipper. These six petals are divided into two groups; three (or apparently two) outer and three inner. One of the inner petals is generally larger, more attractive and different in shape; this is

Below: Odontoglossum luteo-purpureum *and (below right)* Odontoglossum '*Mount McKinley*' *are epiphytic orchids that, given careful attention, can be cultivated as houseplants. Above right:* Paphiopedilum concolor *with its beautifully marked cream flowers.*

the lip (*labellum*). The stamens in orchids are not immediately obvious. In the centre of the flower is a small column (*gynostemium*) consisting of the style and the stamens; two stamens in the Venus' Slipper group but only one in the rest of the Orchidaceae.

For the amateur it is really only possible to propagate orchids by division. *Coelogyne cristata*, *Odontoglossum grande* and *Odontoglossum pulchellum* are propagated by division of the pseudobulbs in the spring when new growth is beginning, with the severed pseudo bulbs placed on a tray of moss. *Paphiopedilum insigne* (Venus' Slipper) can be propagated by detaching young shoots with their own root system from the somewhat older plants and potting them up in a specially prepared compost. Instead of the classic compost for orchids, consisting of *Polypodium*, beech and *Osmunda* roots, increasing use is recently being made of tree-ferns, bark from Finland and California, ground cork oak, perlite, vermiculite, polystyrene granules, charcoal, hard peat varieties and granulated peat.

Paphiopedilum villosum *with its brown-green-white flowers, is cultivated in an ordinary room or greenhouse.*

Hydroponics

Strangely enough, the soilless cultivation of plants was already known to the Greeks at the dawn of history, but it was not until after the Second World War that this fascinating method of growing plants came into its own. Hydroponics, which literally means 'water work' is not, however, strictly true since the plants are really grown in a nutrient solution. The enthusiasm of a Berne nurseryman, one G. R. Vatter, a pioneer in this field, subsequently led to its widespread use by the Swiss public. A good deal of interest is also being shown for this method in Germany, Austria and the United States, while in Great Britain and The Netherlands, the number of hydroponic enthusiasts has greatly increased since special companies become concerned with its commercial application. Professional growers are also using the hydroponic system to good effect, especially for the production of tomatoes and carnations, and experimentation continues to take place in research stations.

The first hydropot came from Switzerland and was called Plantanova. It was made of green glass, to prevent the growth of algae, had an inset (inner container) that looked like a coffee filter only with larger holes, and with it we bought a tube of concentrated liquid feed tablets. We still have this pot and it continues to serve us well. A plastic container later appeared on the market, but this had the disadvantage that we could no longer follow the growth of the roots. However, our curiosity was satisfied to a certain extent by lifting out the inset now and then.

The nutrient solution must in any event form a combination of the main element: nitrogen, phosphoric acid and potassium, plus magnesium and essential trace elements. But the plant lover need not bother his head about the chemical composition: he simply uses the end-product.

With the hydroponic system, you start off with young plants, the roots of which have been washed clean of every trace of compost. The base of the inset is covered up to 3–4cms deep with a chemically inert substance (soil substitute) such as natural gravel, vermiculite or one of the newer filling materials. The cleanly rinsed plant or rooted cutting is then carefully placed in the inset and more of the filling is added to anchor the plant in its upright position. Following this, just enough tepid water is poured into the outer container so that a layer of air remains between the inset and the water level. No nutrients are added during the first week. Most hydropots come equipped with a water level indicator of some sort. The idea is that some of the plant's roots grow in the inset, the rest find their way down into the feeding solution.

There are now several new substitutes for gravel on the market, such as expanded clay granules, that have been subjected to intense heat—like popcorn! The advantage of this filling over gravel is that it is light and porous, and so able to both absorb and retain water without rotting or becoming mouldy. Switzerland was the first on the market with Argex-granules. These are previously heated to over 1000°C, which not only makes them extremely absorbent but gives them a good supporting propensity, which also encourages well-knitted roots. Perlite, a white expanded granite product, is also very popular.

Water runs off gravel, which is not the case with clay granules. So it is not surprising that these, and similar substances, are now the chosen filling for all shapes and sizes of hydropots, tubs and troughs. You can choose between finer or coarser granules, depending on the size and type of plant, and it is generally not necessary to renew the feeding solution more than once in two months.

You can now buy a hydroponic unit at a good garden centre, which comes complete with plant and precise instructions. The advantages of one particular hydropot we have seen is that it has a large water reservoir and has managed to dispense with the need for a water level indicator, which can often prove faulty in the conventional pots and troughs, and it, too, comes complete with plant. With this ready-made system there is no need to wash the compost from the roots, neither is it necessary to pot up. The

*Top: A hydropot of green glass.
Above: Bedded in washed clay granules, the plant is placed in the inside container.*

unit consists of a pot made of synthetic material, sharply narrowed at the base, around and at the bottom of which are slit openings, through which the roots grow. This pot is filled with expanded clay granules that support the plant. The narrower base part of the pot fits neatly into a round opening in the wider-based water reservoir, which is 4cms high and contains 6½ dl water. This water container has only a small opening on top for filling, which stops evaporation and discourages the growth of algae. The roots reach the water reservoir through the slits. No liquid feed is necessary during the first week, and after this a suitable proprietary liquid feed, diluted in water, suffices. With this system, the reservoir can become almost empty before it needs to be topped up. Maintenance is simple: rinse the clay granules clean and renew the nutrient solution every three months. This product of Dutch ingenuity should soon be more widely available, so it is perhaps worth making enquiries.

There are special, large hydro troughs and tubs made for a mixed group of plants which are very popular for offices, showrooms, factories and the like, where they form a much appreciated decoration. These can be made of asbestos-cement (waterproofed), earthenware (Spanish red containers, for example), plastic and various other synthetic materials. The best plants for these containers are those that have been previously raised in little black plastic pots set in a nutrient solution, which adapts them to soilless cultivation from the very start so they can be safely potted on in clay granules. They are placed, pot and all, in a trough or tub, with the customer choosing a combination of plants on the spot. The plant-trough should be 20–24cms deep. With the exception of cacti (who like their pots wide and low), these plants are happiest in their moist substrate and damp atmosphere, where they will flourish to perfection. They are then often given a nutrient solution of 20cc to 10 litres of water.

There is also a system (known on the Continent as the Maarse-sytem) that is often called semi-hydroponics, although this definition is not really correct, since the plants actually stand in soil. These containers can be bought in various garden centres. The plants are often bedded in a mixture of leafmould with 10% hygro-meal. The bottom of the container is first covered with a thick layer of clay granules (7–10mm) in a nutrient solution, on which is placed a 'feed blanket' (a filter mat made of synthetic material). Then follow the plants in the aforementioned compost and the surface is covered with clay granules. Use is made here of a filling tube and a water level indicator. The latter must register green at all times. It will be necessary to top up with water during the first two weeks. Whatever your choice, all garden centres will provide information about the various hydroponic systems, pots, manner of planting and the appropriate nutrient solutions. In England, the House of Rochford at Hoddesdon, Herts, is one of the leading distributors of hydroponic systems.

Plants are now also being grown in rockwool with a nutrient film. This is a new method, used mainly in tree nurseries for raising cuttings and in the florist trade for growing carnations and chrysanthemums. At a recent exhibition we saw good results with cyclamens that had been grown in rockwool containing a nutrient solution. This system, however, is still largely confined to commercial growers. The difficulty here is that little moisture is released, which can sometimes result in rotting. But all these new methods are worth mentioning, and it is nice to be an informed visitor at a horticultural show!

Top: Plastic suction-pump for emptying a hydro-trough. Centre: The water level is visible through a small glass panel in the side of the pot. Above: A new hydroponic method— plastic pots with their own self-watering system.

Flowering bulbs in the home

A windowsill glowing with an array of flowering bulbous plants during the bleak days of winter is no longer a rarity, and the range of specially prepared bulbs of good quality has consequently become much larger in recent years. However, the early flowering 'forced' varieties available around the Christmas holidays are more limited: some early small tulips, cluster narcissi (the so-called Paperwhites) and the specially prepared early flowering hyacinths. One difficulty is finding a good storage place, since potted bulbs need to spend a fair time in a cool, dark room. And where do you find such a place in a house that is centrally heated from top to bottom? Happily, the arrival of plastic put an end to this particular problem, and now even a dark cupboard in a moderately heated room is suitable. First water the bulbs in their pots, bowls or jars and then wrap them in a plastic bag. Check regularly to see they have sufficient moisture, and when the 'noses' are long enough, move the bulbs into the light of a warm room, but leave the plastic cover on for a few more days.

However, storing in the garden is still the best method. Dig a shallow pit in a shadowy spot, place the bulbs in their pots and bowls in the pit, and cover the whole pit with a layer of earth at least 5cms deep. Bulbs can stand cold

Below: Tulip bulbs. Bottom: A hyacinth growing in a special glass jar. Right: Hyacinthus *hybrid* '*Blue Jacket*'.

but not frost, so when this threatens, protect them with an additional generous layer of fallen leaves or dry peat. Leave them for at least two months, then check whether the shoots are 6–8cms long. If this is not the case, cover them up again with a thicker layer.

As the flowering period of the diverse bulb plants and their strains varies to a certain extent, we would refer you to the appropriate plant descriptions arranged in alphabetical order at the back of the book. For the small bulbous and corm plants we would suggest *Crocus* and *Scilla*. If you would like something different, then we would recommend *Haemanthus* (Bloody Lily or Fireball), *Hippeastrum* (Amaryllis), *Hymenocallis*, *Vallota* (Scarborough Lily) and *Veltheimia*. These more unusual plants are not as readily available as the traditional winter flowerers and the initial outlay will be costlier, but against this they will last for many years and one bulb per pot is enough for a splendid display. (See also: Monthly calendar.)

Far left: Crocus *hybrid. Centre left:* Scilla-non-scripta, *Squill, a wild star hyacinth. Below left:* Veltheimia capensis *or Forest Lily. Left:* Haemanthus multiflorus (*Salmon Blood Lily*). *Below: The* Hippeastrum reticulatum *strain* 'Stratifolium' *or* 'Candy Cane'.

Bottle gardens

*Below: Inserting the drainage layer and compost by means of a cardboard funnel is an exacting job. Centre: The plants are planted in the soil.
Bottom: A decorative 'garden in a bottle'.*

The 'garden in a bottle' has now definitely achieved pride of place in a large number of homes. Arranging your own miniature garden in a large glass container or bottle is a fascinating occupation that gives full rein to a plant lover's creative flair. In their glass habitat the plants are sufficiently protected from too dry an atmosphere in the room, drying out of the soil, temperature changes, the adverse effects of smoke, draughts and the harmful vapours given off by a gas stove. Regular watering is also no longer necessary, since the bottle forms, as it were, its own well-balanced microclimate. Water in the compost is taken up by the plants and given off into the surrounding atmosphere by the leaves; condensing on the glass, this water then runs back into the soil. In most cases it is only necessary to moisten the compost once every six months. Dirty bottles can be cleaned by rinsing them out thoroughly with water or vinegar mixed with a little sharp sand or uncooked rice. Water mixed with some kitchen salt is also a good cleaning agent, and any stubborn marks on the inside can be got at with a damp sponge pushed through a loop at the end of a long, flexible wire. Give the bottle a really good final rinse with lots of clean water and dry the inside very carefully. When the bottle is absolutely clean and dry (a golden rule), you then pour in a layer of drainage material, such as fine gravel, expanded clay granules or crocks, to a depth of 2–3cms. Do not simply drop this material into the bottle or it might crack the glass. It is best to use a funnel inserted into the top of a cardboard tube, or you could improvise with a carefully rolled newspaper that reaches to the bottom of the bottle. Even then it is wise to tilt the bottle sideways and gently slide the drainage material down. Then add the layer of soil mixture in the same manner, and good results have been achieved with a mixture of two parts leafmould to one part peat dust and one part sharp sand. Ready-made peat-based compost, available at florists, seed merchants, garden centres, and so on, also forms a good base. But whether you choose a loam- or peat-based compost depends on the plants you are planning to use. If you intend to plant ferns or bromelias, then add a little sphagnum moss to the mixture. You can create interest by adding a decorative border of marble chippings, clay granules or lumps of granite or by building up the soil to create a miniature 'landscape' effect.

In order to lower the plants safely through the bottle's narrow neck you will need some specially adapted implements, which you can either buy or make yourself. A plastic spoon, with a handle long enough to make holes in the compost for the plants, is a handy tool and you can use two such spoons to lower the plants into position. A length of bamboo cane, split at one end to form 'tweezers' is also useful for this purpose, and you can tamp down the soil around the positioned plants with a cotton reel firmly wedged onto the other end of the cane, or use the rounded side of the plastic spoon.

When planting, it is best to start at the outside edge and work towards the middle. Place the low-growing plants on the outside, the centre being used for taller plants, and an interesting display can be created by choosing contrasting leaf colours and shapes. It is advisable to start with small plants, and when they are firmly planted, mist the leaves with a fine spray or watering can. If it later becomes necessary to remove a dead leaf or rotted growth, this can be done with a razor blade secured to the end of a cane; it is also useful for any eventual pruning or trimming work.

If the bottle is sealed too soon after planting, then, inevitably, so much condensed moisture will form on the inside of the glass that the plants will be obscured from view. It should therefore be left unsealed until a balance has been reached between the temperature and atmosphere inside and outside the bottle. This can take a few weeks. If a sealed bottle still produces too much vapour, then remove the stopper immediately and try again a week or so later. The correct level of humidity has been reached when the glass remains clear. Considering the ideal growing conditions which are created in a bottle, it is wise to choose slow-growing and dwarf plant species. Apart from bottles with a narrow neck, you can also create miniature gardens in a goldfish bowl, wine flagon, carboy, glass dome, aquarium or terrarium.

Light, air and water

Light

Without light no plant growth! Lack of light is therefore often the reason why, in spite of the best of care, some plants still fail to flourish. In this case, they should be moved to a lighter position or given extra artificial lighting.

The amount of light a plant needs

depends on the conditions it enjoyed in its country of origin: ground-covering plants originating in tropical forests have naturally adjusted themselves to less light than, for instance, our heath plants. Green foliage plants—the so-called shade plants—need less light than the variegated leaf or flowering plants. The same applies to plants during their winter dormant period, when they require less light than the growing and flowering specimens. The crucial role of light in a plant's growing process is clearly illustrated by observing plants that flower in late autumn: bud development stops as soon as the days become noticeably shorter. At this time all overwintering houseplants have to

contend with less light.

As daylight in the average home generally comes from one side only, a plant, which naturally turns towards the light, will soon adjust itself totally to its situation. This means that the plant must not only be given the correct position, but should also be allowed to keep it! It

is not a mere object, like a piece of furniture that we can shove around at will, but a living creation that becomes attached to its own 'spot'. Even a quarter turn of the pot is detrimental to some plants; an Azalea, for instance, cannot tolerate it at all! The *Camellia*, *Epiphyllum* (*Phyllocactus*) and *Zygocactus* (Christmas Cactus) are particularly sensitive to being moved or turned and will often drop their flower buds if shuffled about. It is therefore better to tend your plants on the spot, and if you have to move them from the windowsill for a short time, put them back in the same position, marking the side of the pot and its situation. One particularly persistent fallacy is that plants should stand in the sun.

Foliage begonias, palms and ferns cannot tolerate direct sunlight at all, although they do, of course, need light. A north-facing window is ideal for them, and is a position, incidentally, that suits all shade plants. Most houseplants appreciate a little morning sun, coming in from an east-facing window, for example. Strong midday sun, on the other hand, is nearly always deadly: trapped behind glass, the vast majority of plants become uncomfortably hot, and the risk of scorching is considerable. This poses quite a problem in many apartments where the living room faces south. In the individual plant descriptions you

will therefore often see the advice: protect from the midday sun. You can do this simply by placing a newspaper or folding plastic screen between the plants and the glass, or by drawing your net curtains, if you have them. Outside adjustable awnings or slatted shutters are, of course, ideal since they also keep the increasing heat of the sun out of the room. Failing this, Venetian blinds, with adjustable slats for letting in variable amounts of sunlight, and plastic, paper or cane roller blinds, also work very well—especially the split-cane or bamboo type, because they filter the light. Their natural colour also harmonises well with plants, and they are comparatively inexpensive. But whatever screens you use, it is important to close them only for the few hours of direct, strong sunlight, otherwise your plants will suffer from lack of daylight!

A really dark spot in the house is not really suitable for a plant. But you can try it out with the climbers *Cissus antarctica*, *Philodendron scandens*, *Rhaphidophora aurea* or *Syngonium*. All four would feel a good deal better, though, if you compensate for the lack of daylight with some extra artificial lighting.

We have discovered from personal experience that flowering plants continue to develop their buds if they are placed for 16 hours or more under a 60 Watt lamp with a reflector, hung 80cms above the plant—or above the tallest plant in a plant-trough—but combined with a temperature of 20°C. (This applies especially to *Impatiens*, *Pelargonium*, *Saintpaulia* and *Streptocarpus*.)

We saw really luxurious growth in a plant-trough that stood at least 4 metres from a window, but had a 100 Watt lamp suspended 1 metre above it throughout the entire year. The height of such a spotlight can vary from 40–100cms, depending on the available daylight, and a reflector has the advantage of utilising the light to the maximum. The rather 'playful' looking hanging unit, consisting of the two halves of a ball joined together with lengths of chain, also works very well: the bottom half holds the plant and the top half conceals a 15 Watt bulb (not stronger, otherwise the leaves will scorch). Fluorescent tube lighting, with its rather stark effect, is less suitable for the living room, but it has the advantage of spreading light more evenly and it does not radiate heat.

Air

Plants detest draughts but they do like fresh air. It is therefore necessary to air a room regularly, not only for our own benefit but also for our plants. Dry air is also harmful, and always becomes something of a problem when the colder weather arrives—particularly with central heating—because most plants require a moist atmosphere. Investing in a hygrometer (which measures the moisture content of the air) is therefore no luxury for the true plant enthusiast. When the indicator on this useful instrument falls below 70, spraying is necessary.

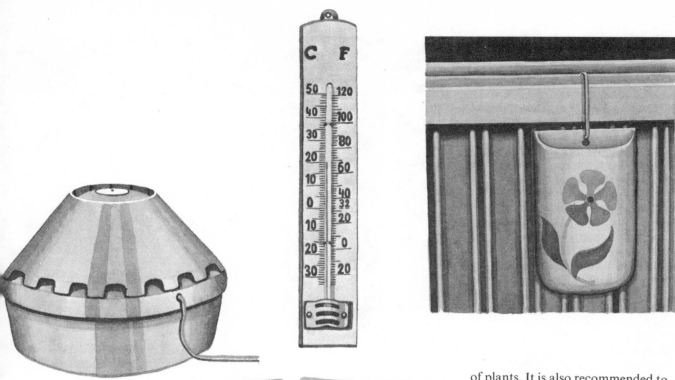

of plants. It is also recommended to widen the windowsill above the radiator, so that the rising warm current of air will not pass directly along the pots and leaves.

Temperature
Great changes of temperature are very detrimental to a plant, and during the winter especially, plants are often given a harder time than is necessary. During this season there are often very warm and very cold rooms in one and the same house. When night falls and the heating is

Tropical plants needing a constant humid atmosphere can be placed on slats laid across a container of water, or on an upturned saucer in a dish of water. Several plants can be combined in a tray of moist peat or on a bed of wet pebbles, without the bottom of the pots touching the water. Large ferns and arums can also be plunged into a second container packed with moist peat. All these methods are intended to surround your houseplants with the moist atmosphere they enjoyed in their original environment. The drier the air, the greater the chance of shrivelled leaf tips and leaf-fall. This is why a water container hung on the radiator or special humidifiers—available at garden shops or centres—are really a necessity. An automatic electric humidifier or mister will render invaluable service in a room containing a large number

turned down low, the temperature near the windowsill drops far too quickly for the comfort of the plants. Again, they are simply supposed to get used to it!

The first problems begin when the plants that have spent the summer in the garden or on the balcony are brought indoors. This tends to happen far too suddenly; as soon as we hear the first warning of frost, they are rushed indoors, straight from the fresh air into a warm room behind glass! It is a wonder that they survive at all. Such plants should be given a sporting chance to acclimatise. Place them first in an unheated but sunny room that is aired daily, at a temperature of 10–15°C. Other norms apply to the so-called conservatory plants that spend the summer outdoors in tubs or other large containers, but because of their limited winter hardiness, need to overwinter in a frost-free but cool environment. A temperature of 5–8°C is sufficient, for example, for *Nerium oleander*, *Agapanthus*, *Agave americana*, *Camellia*, *Lantana*, *Citrus* species, laurels, pomegranates and nearly all fuchsias. During the winter the majority of tropical plants require a day temperature of 18–22°C, not falling below 15°C at night. For stronger plants a night minimum of 10–12°C is sufficient, even for *Coleus* and *Hoya*.

The winter flowerers among our houseplants will generally not thank you for a high temperature and a dry atmosphere. Various winter-flowering begonias are quite happy at 12–15°C, and an *Azalea indica* in bud is even content with 6–10°C, as is *Crassula portulacea* and *C. arborescens*. *Euphorbia fulgens* and *E. pulcherrima* like warmth and prefer a temperature of 18–20°C.

Water

Water is the source of life for every plant. Of course, everyone who keeps plants knows this, but the eternal question remains: how often and how much? It would be nice if we could give a general answer to this question, but there simply isn't one. Here, too, different plants have varying water requirements that are, moreover, dependent on the season and on the location. Plants lose a lot of their moisture through transpiration during the summer, and this needs to be taken into account when watering. It is best to water

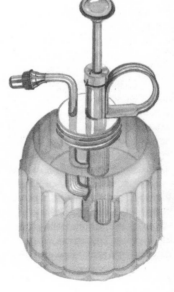

44

your plants early in the morning, as this will sustain them against the heat of the day. If the soil of some specimens feels dry again by evening, then go ahead and give them a second watering! Spraying the leaves of foliage plants can also have a refreshing effect. It is better for cacti to be dry again before evening, but during particularly warm days they can be included in the early morning watering round, over their crown. Overwintering plants should never be watered if the soil is still moist and dark in colour.

And plants that spend the winter in a cool, frost-free room need very little

water (once a week will generally suffice), while flowering plants in a heated room should be watered every day. Tropical plants should also be checked daily, but do not water too liberally; if the surface is dry, examine the undersurface by pushing your finger into the soil. Cacti, with the exception of the leaf cacti, can do without water entirely between November and March (at a temperature of 10°C maximum), and plants that drop all their foliage in the autumn can also remain dry during the winter. These include *Achimenes*, *Sinningia*, *Rechsteineria* and *Hippeastrum* (10–12°C). Most plants dislike wet feet, so any water that drains through the soil into the saucer (or into the ornamental outer container) after watering should be removed after 30 minutes. This water cools down too sharply, and cold water is never good for the roots of the houseplant, not even in the summer. It is therefore important always to have water at room temperature to hand. Make a habit of refilling the watering can as soon as it is empty and leave it standing in the same, fairly warm place, then you can be sure that the water will always be at the right temperature. As far as your watering can is concerned, apart from aesthetic considerations as to its shape and colour, choose one

with a good long spout that can reach under the foliage direct to the soil without spilling.

Ways of increasing the atmospheric humidity in a room are described on page 42. Information about pots and containers with a built-in watering system can be found on pages 57–8.

Another difficulty is the quality of the water. Everyone is aware that rainwater is the best thing for houseplants. It is, in fact, rather acid, which is something most plants like. It is also soft and reasonably pure—that is, if you don't happen to live in an out-and-out industrial area! Most plant-lovers, however, will probably have their own ingenious methods of catching the falling raindrops (but not, we hope, via a tarred or asphalted roof, since particles of tar or asphalt are deadly for plants!). Unfortunately tapwater can be far from ideal for plants. It often contains a high content of magnesium salts, chlorine and/or a high salt content, as well as a generous portion of lime, which causes hard water. For true lime-loving plants such as *Aspidistra*, *Campanula isophylla* and *Hoya* varieties, this is hardly a disadvantage. But the majority of houseplants dislike lime, which we continue to add to the compost with every libation of water! Consequently, an agglomeration of mineral salts gradually builds up in the compost. The correct acid level (pH) is disturbed and progressively declines (the current proprietary composts have a pH value of $5\frac{1}{2}$). We should, therefore, use every means to prevent the effect of calcification on our houseplants. When we see this as a

chalky white crust on the outside of a porous clay pot, it is sometimes too late. White chalk blotches on leaves (a result of spraying and sponging) or a hard, white crust on the soil surface are equally ominous warnings. All clear evidence that the water department has been adding too much lime and magnesium to its water supply; consequently the degree of hardness of such water is much too high (more than 12 degrees). You can find out the degree of hardness of your water supply by contacting your local water board. Special water-softeners can be purchased from hardware stores and large supermarkets, or tapwater can be boiled to soften it temporarily. For acid-loving plants put a ball of peat fibre in a muslin bag and leave it hanging in a bucket of water overnight; the humic acids of the peat will restrain the particles of lime. You can also buy reasonably inexpensive water-filters that screw onto a tap. These supply as much distilled water as you want, but for ease of use it is advisable to have an extra tap installed. If you decide to purchase one of the chemical water softeners, make sure the information on the packet expressly states that the product is suitable for houseplants. The well-known domestic products that produce 'soft' water for rinsing clothes and those that deter chalk from forming in the washing machine are certainly not suitable!

Gloss and feeding

Leaf gloss
In the days of open fires, stoves, brooms and dustpans it was necessary to sponge large-leafed plants constantly in order to remove the dust. Nowadays, when so many homes have central heating and a vacuum cleaner, the need for so much

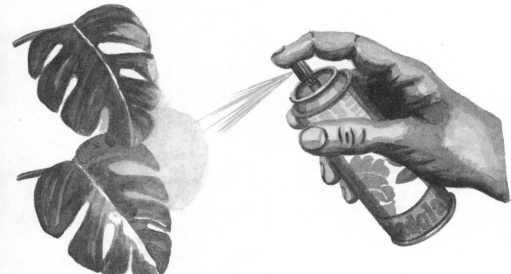

dusting is largely a thing of the past. Some 'enthusiasts' used to polish the leaves of their plants with a piece of cotton wool soaked in oil or milk, but this closes the pores and endangers the plant.

The manufacturers then came up with leaf gloss. It was first used by florists, who sprayed their large-leafed plants to a brilliant shine before displaying them to potential customers. We were a little wary of this at first, but foliage gloss products have since proved themselves to be reliable and welcome aids to the plant-lover. They are now on the market in small sizes, as aerosols, sprays, or as a liquid which you smear onto the leaves with a sponge. Dusting and sponging becomes superfluous, and leathery-leafed plants acquire a natural high gloss effect. These gloss products also help to keep the plants healthy, and contain a substance that makes water and chalk marks disappear. The leaves should be sprayed from a distance, otherwise they can suffer from the effects of freezing. Do not

treat your plants with any gloss more than once every 3 or 4 weeks. And always read the instructions for use on the canister or bottle.

Houseplant foods
A plant is self-supporting: it makes its own food. The roots take up water and mineral salts from the soil, the leaves absorb carbon dioxide from the air. Using sunlight as its source of energy, the plant converts these three raw materials into carbohydrates and proteins. This process releases oxygen into the air, so, in fact, a houseplant is as beneficial to man as a tree.

We can supplement the plant's natural food with houseplant

fertiliser. As a rule, plants are only fed in the spring and summer, when they are in active growth. A plant should never be fed in its resting period or if it is ailing. Flowering plants benefit from a weekly application of houseplant fertiliser, and foliage plants generally respond well if they are sprayed every 2 weeks with a leaf fertiliser; the food is taken up through the leaves and carried to all parts of the plant. Plants that like an acid soil (bromelias, ferns and other woodland plants) can be given an organic fertiliser, or you can alternate with an organic and a chemical fertiliser.

The firm of Jiffy have recently introduced an ingenious product that both waters and feeds the plant from under the pot. It consists of two artificial resin discs, a year's supply of chemical plant-food granules and a filter-wick (an absorbent tape). You make an indentation in one of the discs with your thumb, put in the granules and cover them with the second disc. This unit is then placed in the bottom of a decorative container or drainage saucer. You then push the wick up to half of its length through the drainage hole under the plantpot, pushing a pencil up through the hole to make a space. The plantpot with the wick projecting is finally placed on the disc unit, and water is then added to the decorative container or drainage dish. The resin discs absorb this water, thus activating the food granules. You can add more water, but make sure that the water level remains just below the bottom of the plantpot. The plant will now take up only as much water and food as it needs, just as it does in nature! It will be necessary to add water from time to time, but there is enough food present for an entire year. With this method you should never water directly onto the compost.

Pruning and repotting

Pruning

In February we should rouse our houseplants from their winter sleep. They are then often sorely in need of a good grooming session! We discover withered leaves, bare stems, lank, sluggish plants that have clearly suffered from lack of light, specimens that have somehow been allowed to grow wild, and a few whose roots are growing through the drainage hole.

What do we do with them?

Begin with some careful pruning. A necessary operation if we wish to rejuvenate and restore to their natural shape plants that have shot up too high or have grown too wide. Remove the long, straggling sideshoots from climbing plants to keep them within desired limits. This cutting back, however, should not be done at random. Care should be taken to ensure that the plant is restored to its correct shape: don't simply cut all the branches off at the same level with big pruning shears, but handle them carefully one by one. On the other hand, don't be afraid of taking a resolute grip on the pruning knife, for a couple of inches either way will not constitute a tragedy! Snip the tops off smoothly one at a time, but always just above an eye or a leaf axil growing in the direction in which you want the plant to develop. Keep the prunings—they can be used as cuttings. Use a very sharp knife and make the cut clean and straight.

Which plants should we prune?

All the bushy plants that are showing superfluous growth, have entangled branches, or have become bare towards the base.
Further: *Ampelopsis* (Virginia Creeper), *Beloperone* (Shrimp Plant), *Bougainvillea*, *Coleus* (Flame Nettle), *Dipladenia*, *Fuchsia*, *Gardenia*, *Hibiscus* (Rose of China), *Iresine*, *Pachystachys*, *Pelargonium* (Geranium), *Plectranthus*, *Pilea*, *Plumbago* and *Stephanotis*.

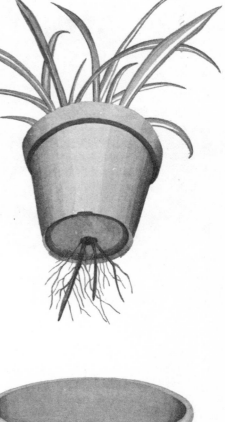

Repotting

Plants that are pruned in February–March can also be given fresh compost and, if the roots are growing through the drainage hole, a bigger pot. A new clay pot should first be soaked in a bucket of water for 24 hours so that it is thoroughly saturated before you use it. Small peat pots should likewise be really well moistened. As a rule the new pot should be one, or even two, sizes larger than the old one. Cover the drainage hole with 'crocks' (a broken piece, or pieces, of pot or brick), rounded side up. Plants that prefer light, airy soil (orchids, *bromelias*, *Anthurium*) need a good layer of crocks; with orchids you can even fill a third of the pot with them. Plants that have been raised in plastic pots should be repotted in the same. Crocks are not strictly necessary here, but always make sure that no drainage water is left standing in the saucer or at the bottom of the outer container. Plastic pots are ideal for cacti and succulents, since the bottom remains warm.

Not any old pot will do! The current plantpots—made of clay or plastic, available in a range of sizes—are suitable for the majority of houseplants. But surface-rooting plants, such as Azalea, *Cyperus* and *Sansevieria*, need a different model: wider and relatively rather shallow. Palms like a tall, narrow pot. But whatever pot you choose, make sure that your plant will be at relatively the same level it was in its former pot, as planting too deep can cause root rot. The compost should not be pressed down too hard, particularly if it contains peat moss, since this impairs proper aeration. Carefully remove the old compost from the outer surface of the soil-ball, spread a layer of fresh compost on the eventual drainage crocks, gently lower the plant into its new pot and gradually add more compost around, and finally over, the soil-ball. Press down firmly with the fingers or a wooden dibber to about 1–2cms below the rim of the pot to avoid spillage when watering. It is still possible to repot and renew the compost of pot-bound plants right through the summer, for a plant is ready for repotting when the roots are visible through the drainage hole.

This is also the case when the entire surface of the pot is criss-crossed with young shoots, something that often happens with, among others, *Anthurium, Calathea, Clivia, Cyperus, Maranta, Sansevieria* and various bromelias.

Pruned and repotted plants are not a particularly attractive sight, but we must give them time to revive. Place newly-repotted plants in a light, warm situation, but definitely not in full sunlight.

Composts

The traditional compost used by florists was generally based on three parts leafmould, two parts rotted cow manure (humus) and one part sharp sand (pure river sand). The pre-packed compost now commonly available in the shops is mainly based on peat with added chemical fertiliser and trace elements. Most ready-to-use manufactured brands are pre-tested nowadays, so there is

no need to mix or sterilise. The John Innes range of composts, available in a number of grades adapted to the maturity stage of the plants, is suitable for most houseplants. But the present range of pre-packed potting composts is so large that it is recommended that you check whether a particular product has been officially tested, and indeed whether it is suitable for your specific requirements. Any good garden centre will advise you on this. Some plants like a little clay or loam worked into the compost, such as *Allamanda*, *Aloe*, *Anacampseros*, *Campanula isophylla* (Italian Bellflower) and *Nerium oleander*. Orchids are happiest with only sphagnum moss, fern roots and sometimes a little beech-leafmould. There is a special potting compost for acid-loving plants (John Innes, among others), as well as cactus compost (non-acid). Leafmould can be made by raking together a heap of fallen leaves and turning them a few times during the year. In order to step up the decaying process you can also add a thin layer of compost-maker now and then. Beech leafmould is the richest in nutrients. Oak leafmould is harmful, particularly for primulas. Sharp sand, the so-called builder's sand, comes from rivers and is added to all composts to aid drainage by aerating the soil, and sphagnum moss, which comes from the peat districts, is an excellent water retainer. Chopped fine, it is mixed with the lighter composts. Fern roots consist of the finely chopped fibrous root systems of various woodland ferns such as *Osmunda* and *Polypodium*.

If you like to have a bag of potting compost handy for use, keep it in a shady, not too dry, place.

Pokon Products have recently introduced a new dehydrated, instant potting compost: small, handy blocks, that swell up to $1\frac{1}{2}$ litres of fresh potting soil when mixed with 1 litre of water.

Propagation

The true plant-lover will invariably want to increase his or her own stock of houseplants, particularly when they discover just how rewarding home propagation can be. The various methods (cuttings, division, air-layering and seed sowing) are as follows:

Cuttings

The simplest method of growing roots on a cutting is still: put it in a bottle of water. Moreover, you have

the added pleasure of actually seeing the roots grow! Choose a fresh tip or sideshoot 6–10cms long from the most vigorous growth of the plant and cut cleanly across just beneath a node, the point where the leaf is attached to the stem. Remove the lower leaves from the cutting and place it in a bottle of water, but make sure that the base of the cutting does not touch the bottom of the bottle. Roots have the best chance of developing about halfway down the bottle.

As soon as the cutting has grown a nice show of healthy roots it can be planted in ordinary potting compost. However, if after two weeks there are still no roots visible, you can try planting the cutting in peat fibre leafmould, or a proprietary rooting medium.

Suitable plants for this method are *Aphelandra*, *Begonia corallina*, *B. metallica*, *B. semperflorens*, *Coleus*,

Cyperus, *Fuchsia*, *Gynura*, *Hedera*, *Hypoestes*, *Impatiens*, *Iresine*, *Nerium oleander*, *Passiflora*, *Pilea cadierei*, *Plectranthus*, *Rhaphidophora aurea*, *Scindapsus pictus*, *Setcreasea* and *Tradescantia*.

Alternatively, you can root your cuttings directly in a suitable cutting compost. After stripping the lowest leaves from a healthy, leafy shoot 6–10cms long, insert the base of the cutting firmly 2cms deep into a moist proprietary cutting compost or your

own mixture of equal quantities of peat fibre and sharp sand or leafmould and sharp sand.

Dipping the base of the cutting into a so-called 'hormone type' rooting powder will encourage a more rapid root development. This is best done by first dipping the end of the cutting in water, shaking off any excess droplets and then dipping it 1cm deep in the rooting powder. Using a pencil or stick, you then make a hole in the soil and gently insert the cutting, so that the powder is not shaken off. You can, of course, give each cutting its own separate little pot, but they tend to root sooner and more vigorously if, say, five cuttings are inserted around the rim of, for instance, a geranium pot. *Pelargonium* (Geranium) cuttings should be left to dry out for a few hours before they are put into the compost, otherwise they can easily rot. This also applies to cacti and succulent cuttings. They also like to have their feet planted firmly in plastic pots (warmer!) and require a special cactus rooting medium, available at most garden shops and centres. Sunshine is to be avoided during the rooting process, but they do need to be kept warm.

The potted cuttings should first be watered, then covered with a

polythene bag and secured with a rubber band. You can, if necessary, use a length of wire or four canes to prop up the bag on the inside, thus making a 'mini greenhouse'. Place the pot in a warm, light situation, but avoid direct sunlight! The rooting medium should be kept moist at all times; check after 3 or 4 weeks, and water again if necessary. The appearance of new growth indicates rooting has taken place, and only then should the cuttings be gradually released from their plastic cover so that they can acclimatise to the dry atmosphere of the living room.

The use of polythene bags has proved to be less suitable for propagating

geranium cuttings.

There are also plants that root easily if we use sections of the stem. In this way, several cuttings can be cultivated from one stem. Plants that lend themselves well to this are, among others, *Cissus, Cordyline terminalis, Dracaena, Fatshedera, Fatsia, Hedera, Passiflora, Philodendron scandens, Rhaphidophora, Rhoicissus, Scindapsus, Stephanotis* and *Syngonium.*

The stem sections must have at least 3 leaves or leaf-buds (eyes). Place them vertically in the rooting compost or lay them horizontally on

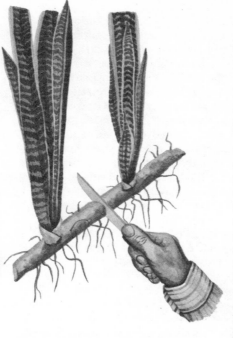

the compost and three-quarters cover them with the soil.

Ficus elastica (Rubber Plant) and *Pisonia* propagate well from leaf-bud cuttings: one stem section with one leaf-bud.

A number of plants can be propagated by means of leaf cuttings. Leaves with a single stalk are inserted upright in rooting medium or peat fibre, and new plantlets will then form at the base of the leaf. This method is applicable to *Peperomia, Saintpaulia,* and *Sinningia. Streptocarpus* can be propagated by removing the central vein of the leaf and placing the leaf halves upright, with their cut edge firmly in peat fibre. With the leaf begonia, *Begonia rex,* you can make several bruises or cuts across the major veins on the underside of the leaf and lay this flat on moistened peat moss or sharp sand, pegging it down with hairpins or weighting

with stones to keep the cut surface in contact with the soil. Small plantlets will eventually develop where the veins have been wounded.

If you wish to have a lot of young *Begonia rex* plants, the leaves can be cut into separate small squares, 1.5 x 1.5cms, and laid flat on the surface of the compost; covering the soil with a thin layer of sharp sand will prevent them damping off. With leaf cuttings the following applies: supply warmth from below and cover with plastic or glass.

The best time to take cuttings from most plants is at the beginning of the growing season in March, but it is possible to do this successfully throughout the entire summer. For woody plants, the best time in the

summer is from the beginning of June to the second half of August. The months of July and August are recommended for leaf-cuttings.

Division

Some plants can be propagated by simply dividing them up into pieces. This is an ideal method for plants that grow from more than one stem, such as ferns, plants that have a rootstock (rhizome) and those that develop offshoots. The first mentioned entails separating the clump of roots into sections by gently teasing them apart, making sure that each separate piece has some top growth attached to it. Plants with rhizomes (an underground stem, acting like a bulb or corm), such as *Sansevieria,* can best be divided by cutting through the root system with a sharp sterilised knife, in such a way that each cutaway section retains at least one shoot as well as a portion of the original root system. Plants with tuberous roots can be treated in the same manner. Plants that develop offshoots—examples of these are *Clivia* and a number of bromelia species—should not be divided until the young plants are half as large as the mother plant.

Air-Layering

A less simple method of propagating plants that are often too woody to root normally. Air-layering is used on plants with a woody stem—*Ficus,* for example—or on a plant that has lost its lower leaves. It is also ideal for shortening a plant that has grown too

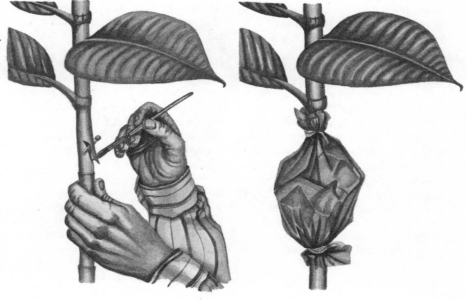

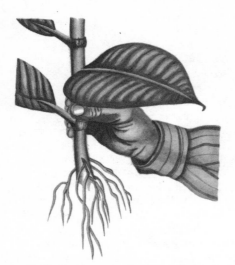

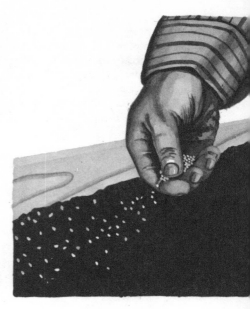

tall. Compact new plants can be produced by making a clean, diagonal cut to the core (about halfway through) of the stem at the place from which you wish it to root. A match should then be placed in the split to prevent it from healing. The split or wound is then smeared with a mixture of rooting powder and lanoline. The treated section is subsequently packed around with dampened sphagnum moss, and finally wrapped in a piece of plastic that is securely sealed at the bottom and the top. Check now and then whether the moss is still moist. When a well-developed root growth is visible through the moss, the packing can be removed. The plant stem is then cut just below the rooted top section, which can now be safely potted up. The plant itself should not be watered over the soil during this period.

Seed Sowing

Raising houseplants from seed is a relatively uncommon practice among home plant cultivators, be it only because you can suddenly find yourself with a host of plants of one and the same species.

Though there is an element of surprise with this method, you never quite know what is going to come up! Seedlings can deviate considerably from the parent plant in both colour and markings, while cuttings will always give you an exact replica of the original plant. Although it is tempting to use seed from your own houseplants, it is recommended that you buy the seed you need from professional nurserymen, since this is taken from the best specimens. Take care not to use old seed, as most seeds do not retain their germinating power for long.

Sow seeds close to the surface so that they are not cut off from the air. As a rule, the thin layer of earth covering the seeds should not be thicker than the seeds themselves, while fine seeds need only be lightly pressed with the finger for they will sift down into the soil by themselves. Seeds need moisture in order to germinate. This is best applied with a spray rather than the spout of the watering can. Ground warmth is absolutely essential. With the seeds of houseplants that are accustomed to overwinter in a cool environment, place a box or tray of small seed pots on the warm mantelpiece or radiator. Tropical plant seeds, however, need a soil warmth of 22–30°C in order to germinate. You can buy an electrically heated propagating tray which is thermostatically controlled at the correct temperature. The seed trays or pots are placed in the tray on a layer of sharp sand, which should be kept moist to ensure an even distribution of warmth and prevent the seedlings drying out. The accompanying seed containers have a plastic cover, complete with a small, sliding air-vent. Ordinary potting compost is not suitable as a germinating medium as it is much too heavy and contains too many nourishing elements. Sieved leafmould or peat fibre mixed with sharp sand is generally used, or you can choose one of a number of proprietary seed composts. In order to retain a suitably humid atmosphere, the entire unit is covered with a sheet of glass or a clear plastic cover. If you use a glass sheet, turn it once daily to remove condensation. As most seeds germinate more easily in the dark, screen the tray with a piece of wrapping paper, and it is best not to remove this paper until you see the first signs of green life. Gradually harden off and aerate the seedlings by propping open the sheet of glass with a piece of wood or, in the case of plastic covers, sliding open the air-vent. The glass sheet should be removed as soon as the growing seedlings touch it.

Now is the time to give your seedlings a little more living space. This means carefully pricking out and transplanting them into boxes or small pots that are again filled with leafmould and sharp sand or a peat-based potting compost. Only when they have again been potted on into

their 'cuttings' pots should you use the appropriate compost for the plant. This pricking out of the minuscule seedlings is a delicate process. Carefully pry up the soil under each seedling with a small fork, and lift it out with the V-shaped end of a stick. Then gently lower the seedlings into the holes—previously made with a sharp pencil or dibber—in the new, moistened compost. These holes should be 5cms apart so that the plants will not be overcrowded when they start to grow. By this method, the following houseplants can, among others, be quite easily raised from seed: *Begonia semperflorens*, *Calceolaria herbeahybrida*, *Capsicum annuum*, *Clivia*, *Coleus*, *Cyclamen persicum*, *Mimosa pudica*, *Phoenix dactylifera* (Date Palm), *Primula sinensis*, *Senecio cruentus* 'Multiflora' (syn. Cineraria), *Solanum capsicastrum*, *Streptocarpus hybridus*.

A number of firms are currently introducing exotic seeds to the market, which are, as yet, only available at garden centres and from seed merchants. The range includes seeds of the species *Acer palmatum* (Japanese Maple), *Arachis hypogaea* (Peanut), *Camellia sinensis* (Tea), *Coffea arabica* (Coffee), *Cordyline indivisa*, *Ficus benjamina*, *Musa ensete* (Abyssinian Banana), *Phaseolus aureus*, *Sparmannia africana* (House Lime or African Hemp), *Yucca aloifolia* (Palm Lily). For the past few years it has been possible to buy inexpensive seed propagators for indoor use (i.e. on the windowsill), complete with a clear plastic cover, peat pots or peat pellets and good F–1 hybrid seeds. Failure is well nigh impossible! With this foolproof apparatus you can raise *Coleus* (Flame Nettle or Painted Nettle), *Pelargonium* (Geranium), *Impatiens* (Busy Lizzie), and even tomato plants, cacti and a number of exotic plants.

Peat seed and cutting pellets (the well-known Jiffy 7's are used mainly for cuttings) are extremely handy to use. They consist of a circular pellet of peat encased in netting, and when watered they swell up to become a real little pot of first-class sowing compost. Always keep the pot moist and place it in a mini-propagating case or under a plastic cover. When the roots are visible through the peat, pot on into suitable potting compost.

Diseases and pest attack

Like all living creatures, plants can also succumb to various diseases and ailments. They then present a truly sorry sight: leaves wilt and fall off, flower buds shrivel and cease to grow. Plants can become the victims of disease or damage caused by infestation of insects, parasites, bacteria, air pollution and poor treatment. The latter in particular is often the reason for many such diseases and ailments. A vigorous, well-tended plant is much more able to withstand a knock or two than one which has become weak as a result of wrong treatment. However, the following information will, we hope, enable you to identify and treat a number of the more commonly occurring plant troubles.

Pests
Houseplants can sometimes fall prey to extremely furtive pest attacks. Spots suddenly appear on the leaves;

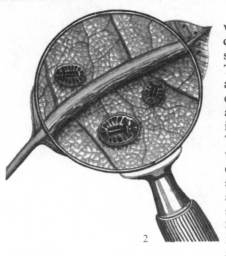

2

matchstick tipped with cotton wool and soaked in methylated spirit. After this treatment the plant should be sprayed regularly with the abovementioned soap-spirit solution. Red spider mites can be treated by spraying the affected plant forcefully and repeatedly, or by giving it a cold

water, after which it should be left to dry out for a while. Ideally the plant should be repotted in fresh compost. Thrips can make their unwelcome appearance in a dry, warm environment, in which case it will almost certainly be necessary to increase the atmospheric humidity. The tiny insects—tan, brown, black with light markings—can be effectively treated with a solution of soft soap, a little methylated spirit and some nicotine (obtained by soaking cigarette butts in water). Spray white flies with the earlier mentioned soap-spirit solution or the above nicotine solution. A radical treatment is to isolate the plant in a polythene bag, into which you spray an insecticide. Being able to identify the specific insect on your plant will assist you in purchasing the right kind of insecticide or pesticide, but if you are at all uncertain, always ask for advice, and always carefully follow the directions on the label.

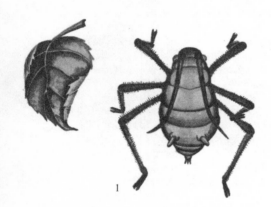

1

3

they feel sticky, lose their lustre, droop and can even fall off, or show a grey webbing or brownish scales. Greenfly (1.), scale insects (2.), mealy bugs, red spider mites (3.), springtails, thrips and white flies (4.).
A harmless domestic remedy for controlling greenfly consists of a solution of 1 litre of water, 20 grammes of soft soap and 10 grammes of methylated spirit. Spray the entire plant forcefully with this solution, and repeat the process every 10–14 days. However, if the intruders are discovered soon enough, a really good spraying with tepid water can effectively wash them away.
Scale insects and mealy bugs can be removed one by one with a

shower or dip several times a week, making sure that the undersides of the leaves are also thoroughly washed. A more immediate remedy is to spray with a vegetable-based insecticide. Placing special plant shafts (available at florists and garden centres) into the soil will also deter attacks by aphids and red spider mites.
Springtails can occur in compost that is kept too moist. Obviously the plant needs to be given less water— also check for correct drainage! Heavy watering drives them to the surface, where they can be seen jumping about like fleas. So the first thing to do is wash them away by bathing the plant in a sinkful of tepid

Jaundice
This disease, which is identified by the yellowing of the leaves, can be caused by any one of the following reasons:
- indigenous plants are placed in too warm a position; move to a cooler location.
- tropical plants have been given a situation that is too cold; move to a warmer spot.
- tropical plants are placed in too dry an atmosphere; spray the leaves, place on an 'island' in water or pack in moist peat.
- a plant is kept in too dark a place; move to a lighter location.
- the plant is suffering from a lack of nutrients; give it fresh compost.

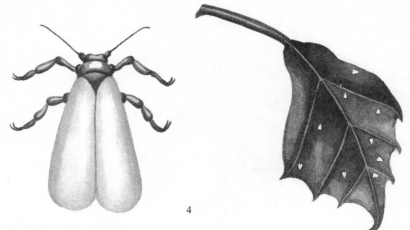

4

- the plant has diseased roots; repot it.
- the plant is being overfed; give it less fertiliser.

Wet feet
It always spells trouble when a plant is left standing with more tepid water in its drainage dish than it can cope with. The shallow pool of rapidly cooling water gives it 'cold feet'. Moreover, this can encourage root-rot with the roots becoming soft, brown and mushy. It is therefore important to remove the unused water and stir up the surface soil so that more air can reach the roots.

Drying out
The leaves turn brown around the edges, and central heating is often the culprit here. The rising hot air is, in fact, detrimental to the majority of houseplants. Sponge large-leafed plants regularly and be generous with the water-spray on the small-leafed specimens.

Stagnation
The plant doesn't 'do' anything! This is a common occurrence. It is possible that the plant simply needs a bit of a rest. If it is otherwise healthy, let it have a break and do not force growth: water very sparingly and do not feed.

Leaf-fall
The causes of this effect are many and varied. It can be that a shade-plant has been exposed to too much sun or has been shifted around too much. Leaf-fall can also be caused by draughts or overwatering, possibly with water that is too cold. Repotting at the wrong time or the shock of transition from a small pot to one

that is much too big, can also result in leaf-fall. Sudden dropping of very many leaves is generally due to a shock to the plant's system, caused by a rapid change in temperature or light intensity. Disease or pest attack can also have the same effect.

Old age
The passage of time leaves its mark on plants as well as people. Vigour and florescence gradually diminish, the leaves become smaller and the distance between them greater. Renew the compost immediately, or try to perpetuate the life of your old plant by taking a final cutting. Then this sad little tale could have a happy ending!

Deformed growth
The plants grow lopsided in the pots and the stately little indoor tree forms a crick in its stem. Set this right by regularly turning the plant, remembering it will turn naturally towards the light source, although it must be said that some plants, namely Azalea, *Camellia*, *Clivia* and *Hibiscus*, will not tolerate this at all. Leaf and phyllo cacti are also very sensitive when the flower buds are developing, and if these plants are turned, their buds will fall off. So let the plants stay exactly where they are and if they do start to grow crooked, support them with a stick.

Root-rot
Roots will rot if the compost in which they grow becomes waterlogged. Improper watering and/or bad drainage can cause

stagnation. The soggy roots will then turn dark brown or even black. The plant's new shoots droop, die off and the entire plant wilts. Severe root-rot is usually fatal but sometimes an infected plant can be saved by removing it from the pot, cleaning all soil from the roots, washing them in warm water, and then repotting the plant in fresh compost. Water very sparingly for a while, until signs of recovery to normal growth are clearly apparent.

Mildew
A fungus disease that can be particularly harmful to plants during the summer which shows itself in the form of a white, powdery mould on leaves. The infection occurs if plants are placed too close together and suffer from lack of air and light, but get too much moisture. The mould can be carefully rubbed off or affected plants can be pruned back, but if the mildew is particularly persistent, the plant should be sprayed with a fungicide. When spraying, do not overlook the undersides of the leaves, but on no account allow the fungicide to touch any flowers.

Green sickness
Deficiency disease, better known as green sickness or chlorosis, is caused because the plant is suffering from a lack of one or more of the essential nourishing elements. The leaves take up insufficient chlorophyll and become light green, yellow and sometimes bleached in colour.

Feeding needs to be correctly adjusted if the plant is to survive.

Frost Danger
Plants standing on the windowsill need to be protected with newspaper during the night when frost is about, especially in rooms where a stove is burning. During a period of sharp frost it is best to remove all plants from the windowsill before you close the curtains, though this is not necessary if your plants are situated above a radiator. Plants standing in an unheated room should not be watered during a frost period, since a wet soil-ball will freeze much sooner than a dry one. If you have to be away for a few days, the plants can be wrapped in an insulating material, such as an old blanket, corrugated cardboard or newspaper and then placed on the floor in the warmest room in the house as far as possible from the window. How can you tell when a plant has been affected by frost? Leaves and stem become translucent and limp, and also change colour from green to dull grey. It is sometimes possible to save a plant by moving it to a dark, cool room and then spraying it thoroughly with cold water. It needs to thaw out very slowly, and if you transfer a frost-bitten plant immediately to a warm room it will have no chance of survival. If a few days after having given it a cold shower there are still no signs of improvement, repeat the process once or twice. Should the plant perk up again, you can begin to adjust it very gradually to a higher temperature.

Plant care during the holidays

If you have a garden, then the best thing you can do is to plunge your houseplants in their pots in a suitably shady spot—but not under dripping trees or shrubs.

When plunging them into their garden bed, make the hole a little deeper than the pot, so that a space remains between the bottom of the pot and the surrounding garden soil. This will prevent harmful insects or excess moisture from entering through the drainage hole. If the weather is dry, soak your plants thoroughly before settling them into their garden bed by immersing them, pot and all, in a bucket of water. As soon as the soil has stopped giving off air bubbles, the pots can be plunged in their sheltered location outdoors.

If your garden is too small, a shady spot on a verandah or patio will serve almost as well. Here the pots should be positioned next to each other against a dividing wall, fence or shed. Give them some support in front, using planks or bricks, to prevent them being blown over by the wind. Drying out is more of a problem when plantpots are not actually bedded in soil, so spray the leaves thoroughly and, again, give the pots a good preliminary soaking in a bucket of water. If you put your plants out on a balcony they will survive better if you plunge them into an outer container (troughs, tubs or orange boxes lined with black plastic) filled with damp peat, but always choose a sheltered position well away from direct sunlight. Delicate and costly plants, such as orchids, bromelias, *Anthurium*, *Aphelandra* and the like, are best lodged elsewhere with a helpful friend.

If you have neither garden nor balcony, and there is no one available to lend a helping hand, your plants can still survive alone at home with a little preparation before you leave. For safety's sake, remove all plants from the windowsill and place them together in the coolest and least sunny room in the house. They should also be thoroughly moistened beforehand, especially if the room has a dry atmosphere. A simple way of making sure that your plants will have sufficient water while you are away is to cover the bottom of a bucket or bowl with a dishcloth in about 1cm of water and place the pots on top. Instead of a dishcloth you can use a layer of crocks or bricks, packed around and above with crumpled pieces of wet newspaper or damp peat. Garden shops also sell special matting on which to stand your pots; this is extremely absorbent, and its capillary action causes the roots to reach down and draw what water they need. Florists have been using it themselves for years.

If you have only a few plants, you can pack them separately in plastic. However, this method is not recommended for plants that are sensitive to damping-off, such as *Begonia rex*, *Pelargonium* and *Saintpaulia*. Large-leafed plants with a single stem can be covered with a polythene bag, closed off just below the lowest leaves.

New houseplant products are in increasing evidence nowadays, and various manufacturers are presently marketing plantpots with a built-in water supply. This self-watering

container is a spring that pushes the inner pot steadily upwards. A tube under the inner pot draws up the required water and also acts as a closing vent. As soon as the inner pot becomes lighter, through lack of water, it is pushed upwards and takes in moisture; conversely, the vent closes when the inner pot has absorbed sufficient water and thus sinks lower again under its own increased weight. The base of the outer container unscrews so that water can be added according to the need of the plant. This sophisticated container is also very suitable for hydroponics, where the soil is replaced by clay granules. Of course, hydroponic cultivation is a completely satisfactory answer to the problem of plant care while you are away on holiday.

system—which gives plants a 3 to 4 weeks supply of water which they take up as they need it—is, of course, extremely beneficial throughout the entire year, but has proven to be a really ideal solution during holiday time. Most of the self-watering products are based on a porous inner container which gradually absorbs the water which is poured between it and an outer container. There are also other systems where the self-watering takes place via a cotton wick or earthenware feeding-column inserted into the drainage hole. Most garden centres supply a number of simple 'self-waterers', some of which come with an adjustable drainage dish. One particularly efficient device consists of a small white column that is inserted into the soil through the drainage hole; it absorbs a surprising amount of water, enough for two weeks, and also contains a generous supply of plant food. You can, moreover, buy an accompanying water reservoir with a filling aperture. The modern plastic pots, complete with drainage rack, air and water reservoir, control window and filling pipe, are also excellent self-watering products that will sustain your plants for at least two weeks. The last word in this field are the fully automatic watering containers that provide a plant with the exact amount of water it needs. Between the inner and outer

But for the very latest plantpots you have to pay the very latest prices, and what usually happens is that we give one or two of our most cherished plants the benefit of a self-watering pot and help the rest to survive in our own particular way. Leave the curtains open when you leave the house, as plants tend to wilt and will also rot sooner in the dark. Blinds or net curtains can be partly closed, particularly if it looks like being a hot summer. Allow fresh air to circulate by leaving the doors of halls and rooms open. If you have ventilators or glass slats in any windows, open them before you leave, so that any rising hot air can escape. A simple watering method that is often used is to pass one end of a woollen thread through the soil of each plant and then place the other end in the bottom of a bucket or bowl filled with water. The plants should then be grouped around the supply bowl, which needs to be placed at the same height as your pots. The water will seep slowly along the thread to the respective pots. In this way they will at least receive enough moisture to prevent them drying out. Strips of lint, tape or even fishing lines can also be used instead of woollen thread.
Cacti and succulents need more water in the summer than during their winter resting period. So this needs

to be taken into account during a prolonged absence. Moreover, at this time the plants need plenty of light and fresh air.
It is fairly difficult for plants and flowers to survive without any attention during a winter holiday. One reasonably efficient way to protect them from draughts and cold is to wrap them in a number of newspapers. But the upper leaves should always protrude from the

protective wrapping. Large plants can be wrapped in blankets. These measures, however, are by no means guaranteed to protect your plants under all conditions, so it is wise to persuade a friend to look in from time to time and look after them if your winter holiday is likely to be a long one.

Monthly calendar

January

Before placing newly-bought houseplants in the living room, give them a transitional period in a moderately warm environment; this helps them to adjust more successfully to their place in your home. When frost is about, it is wise to protect your plants at night by placing some newspapers between them and the icy window. If the room is heated with an open fire or stove, they can, of course, be removed from the windowsill. This is not necessary with central heating, if the radiator is situated under the windowsill.

The Azalea that has been brought into a warm living room from an unheated location in order to bring it into flower now needs to be sprayed regularly over the crown to prevent the developing buds from drying out. Spraying should be stopped once the buds turn colour. The plant should be immersed in a tepid bath once a week to ensure soil moisture.

The winter-flowering, small-flowered *Begonia* requires a light, sunlit location close to a window. Water freely and feed weekly, preferably with a lime-free liquid fertiliser. The Poinsettia (*Euphorbia pulcherrima*) likes a daily spray with tepid water, a warm room and plenty of light and moist air. This way it will flourish at its best. When the flower-like bracts have fallen, cut back the stem 6–7cms above soil level, and staunch the wound with a little white sand, cigarette ash or powdered charcoal, then place the plant in a quiet spot in the room. The newest, more compact strains frequently retain their 'star' bracts and leaves for several months, so cutting back can be happily postponed. Water freely during the growing season to prevent the soil-ball drying out.

The *Camellia* should never be sprayed once the buds have opened, since this makes the flowers sensitive to infection and rot. This plant flourishes best in front of a north- or northeast-facing window. Do not move or turn the pot, otherwise the buds will drop off. To bring the Amaryllis (*Hippeastrum*) into growth and flower, the tuber should

be planted—if this has not already been done in December—up to a third of its depth in lightly pressed compost. Place in a warm position above the radiator or on top of the mantelpiece, and only water the soil around the rim of the pot very sparingly for the first two weeks. With crocuses, first check whether the colour of the buds is visible through the thin membrane. They are then ready to be moved to a warmer location; water freely but make sure that the pot drains well, as too much water may cause root-rot. Berry-bearing shrubs prefer a cool room with plenty of light and a moist atmosphere. Water generously and give the entire plant a good spraying once a week. Foliage plants should be sponged with tepid water every week; ferns and other fine-leafed plants are sprayed. This care not only prevents dust settling but also guards against pest attack. The Christmas Cactus can bloom beautifully at this period, but on no account should it be moved about or turned. Once flowering has ceased, the old blooms can be removed; the plant should not be fed, and only watered very sparingly during this rest period. Winter-flowering succulents— including *Crassula portulacea, Crassula lactea, Echeveria carnicolor*— should receive more water and warmth during the budding and flowering period than at other times. Geraniums, fuchsias and the Bell-flower (*Campanula isophylla*) prefer to spend the winter in a virtually unheated room. It is best not to water them during freezing weather.

February

This is the time to tidy up your *Cyclamen* plant. Carefully twist out any dead flowers and yellowed leaves. Dead growth should not be cut off or tugged at, it will come away from the tuber almost at a touch if it is ready. When the plant has ceased to flower move it to a cooler location; keep the soil fairly dry and stop feeding. The *Clivia*, which should now be in bud, needs to have a flower stem of about 15cms long before being watered freely. Watering before this stage will retard the development of the flower buds.

The *Phyllocactus* in bud should be given a little more water than usual. It will also flower more readily if it is moved to a somewhat warmer location—a well-lit position with a moderate amount of sun. The plant should not be moved or turned during this period, or it is likely to drop its buds. *Nerium oleander* is a plant that tends to lose a lot of its leaves at this time of the year. If this occurs, it is most probably due to a dark, too cool location.

The Gloxinia (also called *Sinningia*), which has been kept dry during the winter, has a tuberous root that can now be potted up in fresh humus soil consisting of woodland soil (leafmould), sharp sand (builder's sand) and rotted cow manure, or you can buy a proprietary peat-based compost and add a little cow manure. The plant should be given a warm location on the radiator or mantelpiece; cover with a sheet of glass or plastic and water moderately to start the growing process.

The same procedure should be followed with the tuber-shaped rootstock of the *Achimenes:* six to eight tubers can be placed in the same pot, but take care not to bed them too deep.

The *Rechsteineria* (*Gesneria,* Cardinal Flower), also responds to the same treatment as the Gloxinia. Overwintering Geraniums, Fuchsias, *Hibiscus, Abutilon, Beloperone* and other shrub-like plants are ready for pruning at the end of this month. Branches that are too long and bare are pruned back to a lower side-branch, but make sure that the cut is made just above a node or healthy shoot. Once the *Bougainvillea* has ceased flowering, the old and dead branches can be removed. The plant needs plenty of sun, light and water; increase the amount of water as soon as the new growth is visible.

March

Now is the time to repot your houseplants; the roots are often to be seen growing through the drainage hole under the pot, and this means that the plant needs a little more living room. The *Clivia* generally needs repotting every two or three years; use this opportunity carefully to remove the young shoots, with some attached roots. These can be planted in a separate pot. The Bellflower (*Campanula isophylla*) is grateful for some fresh compost around this time, and will also respond well to a sunny spot in a heated room.

The flowering Slipper Flower (*Calceolaria*) should be given a cool location. The same treatment applies to the *Senecio* (Cineraria); both species need plenty of water and a fortnightly feed with a nutrient solution. When the Amaryllis (*Hippeastrum*) has finished flowering, it should be treated as follows: cut the flower stem back as far as possible and give the plant water and fertiliser right through the summer. This also applies to the *Veltheimia* when it has ceased flowering.

The *Begonia* that will no longer flower should be cut back to a few centimetres above the soil surface. The summer-flowering *Vallota* has a bulb, which can now be potted up (a third of the bulb should be visible above the soil), then give the pot a position in front of a sunny window in a warm room.

Not too much water. If the plant has overwintered successfully you need only renew the top layer of compost. This also applies to the *Haemanthus*, species of which are commonly known as the Blood Lily and Fireball. The *Haemanthus* prefers to remain in the same container and should not be repotted unless this is obviously necessary. Cuttings of Busy Lizzie (*Impatiens*), *Gynura*, *Pilea*, the Flame Nettle (*Coleus*) and the Rheumatism Plant (*Plectranthus fruticosus*) can be encouraged to form healthy roots if placed in a glass or bottle of water in a warm environment. The cuttings of *Ficus*, *Begonia*, *Aphelandra*, the green and variegated climbers (*Hedera*), *Iresine* and Oleander (*Nerium*) root well with this simple method. With the exception of the *Aphelandra*, they are best given a location in front of a sunny window.

When taking cuttings, cut straight across with a sharp knife just below a leaf joint—the thickened part of the stem from which the new shoots and leaves emerge. Cuttings can also be rooted directly into compost, and with species that show poor progress, it is recommended to help them along with a little hormone powder, which encourages rooting. Various brands are sold at most garden shops or centres. You first dip the end of the cutting in water, then into the powder and finally place it carefully into the cutting compost. Covering with a polythene bag and providing soil warmth will stimulate the root development of most houseplants.

April

The Azalea and *Cyclamen*, having spent some time in a cooler location after their flowering season, may now possibly be plunged out of doors in a cool, shady spot in the garden, if the early spring weather is favourable.

The Poinsettia (*Euphorbia pulcherrima*) is now ready to be brought into growth. If you haven't already done so, cut it back now, unless it is still flowering.

April is also a good time for taking cuttings of the Bellflower (*Campanula isophylla*). Select healthy young shoots about 6–10cms long and insert a number of them around the edge of the pot. This way they should reward you with a new, profusely flowering plant. The Christmas Cactus (*Zygocactus*) should now be stimulated into new growth; if necessary replace the surface with a fresh layer of compost (rich in humus and mixed with sphagnum moss). This plant does not really like to be repotted. Increase the water supply and feed once a fortnight.

Although succulents and cacti that have overwintered in a frost-free environment are liable to grow out of their pots at this time, they are, in fact, happier in their small container. However, if you feel they really need a larger pot, give them one. Plastic pots are ideal for succulents.

The *Bougainvillea* can now be sprayed regularly, until bud formation is clearly evident. The flowering Hortensia (*Hydrangea*) requires a cool position in the room, away from direct sunlight. It needs plenty of water and a weekly feed, preferably with a lime-free nutrient solution.

The *Sansevieria* is now ready for propagation. This is best done by division of the rootstock, which should be carefully cut into several pieces, each of which should have at least one shoot attached. Transplant the portions into pots just large enough to accommodate the roots. Plants that have grown too large need to be divided as and when necessary; such is often the case with, for example, *Anthurium*, the *Maranta* and the Umbrella Plant (*Cyperus*). In order to avoid damaging their delicate roots, some species are best divided under water.

It is now important to give your houseplants some protection from the warm spring sunshine. Plants such as the *Cineraria*, Gloxinia, *Primula*, *Anthurium*, Slipper-flower (*Calceolaria*) and African Violet (*Saintpaulia*), will flourish best if they are given a good light situation but are screened from too bright sunlight.

May

Geraniums should not be watered too copiously; this encourages too much leaf growth which is detrimental to the plant's bud formation. It is better to keep the Geranium indoors until the second half of May, as night frost may still occur at this time of the year. Azaleas that have been plunged in the ground outdoors should now be sprayed daily over the crown if the weather is dry. They also need feeding once a fortnight. The flowering Gloxinia (*Sinningia*) needs to be protected from direct sunlight and watered freely over the soil around the tuber. To provide adequate humidity, it is advisable to place the plant on an 'island' in a dish of water, but make sure that the base of the pot is just above the water level. If you still have cyclamens in the living room, repot them towards the end of May and give them a cool, airy environment. Given the right conditions, they can also be placed in a well-sheltered spot in the garden.

The Busy Lizzie (*Impatiens*) and the *Solanum* (Christmas or Jerusalem Cherry) can likewise be placed outdoors, providing they are given a sheltered position in the shade. Bromelias should be screened from the warm noonday sun; soft water may now be poured into the funnel. The same applies to the *Cryptanthus*, a low-growing member of the bromeliad family, with a flat rosette. Since this species does not have a true funnel, it absorbs water less easily, so make sure the soil-ball does not dry out. It responds well to an occasional feed with a liquid fertiliser diluted in soft water and sprayed over the leaves.

There is still plenty of opportunity for dividing and taking cuttings, especially of cacti and succulents. However, before potting up the latter, allow the sections to dry out for at least a week. Cuttings of the *Opuntia* are best tied to a small stick to prevent them falling over. The Calla or Arum Lily (*Zantedeschia*) is now ready to take its natural resting period (May–July); withhold both water and fertiliser. The foliage can be allowed to dry out almost completely.

The *Hydrangea* that has flowered in the living room in the spring can now be placed out of doors. Cut back the foliage to about 2cms above the old wood (recognisable by its slightly darker tint) and plunge the pot into the ground in a sheltered, well-shaded spot in the garden. Gradually increase watering when new growth appears, and feed regularly.

June

Plants that flourish in a sunny location outdoors, such as the *Bougainvillea*, *Plumbago*, Oleander (*Nerium*) and *Punica granatum*, can now be moved from the house into the garden. Spray regularly and thoroughly over the foliage (that is, unless the plant is still bearing flowers), and continue to feed. Houseplants that are now in full bloom should be fed once a week or once a fortnight.

Cacti and succulents also need nourishment at this time, albeit to a lesser degree; once a month is sufficient for succulents. The more pronounced the fur or spines of the cactus, the more careful one should be about feeding; a proprietary cactus fertiliser is best.

Of course, the amount of sun and warmth needed by different plants varies considerably, but it is a basic fact that the majority of our houseplants cannot tolerate full sun, and this is something we need to keep well in mind as high summer approaches.

However, here too, the exception proves the rule, since the Dwarf Geranium, *Hibiscus* and Oleander, as well as many species of cacti and succulents, tolerate sunlight extremely well. The *Faucaria tigrina* (Tiger's Jaws or Cat's Jaws),

even enjoys full sun; it can bloom throughout the entire year, providing the sun shines. The Passion Flower (*Passiflora*) is also a sun lover, needing plenty of light and fresh air. The climbing or trailing *Hoya* is available in three species: *Hoya bella* is a trailer, with pendulous branches, small pointed leaves and hanging flowers, *Hoya carnosa* (Wax Plant) is a good climber, with larger flowers and egg-shaped leaves; while *Hoya imperialis*, with its rather downy leaves and hanging clusters of reddish-brown flowers with a white centre, is more suitable for the warm greenhouse. It is best not to remove the dead flowers, since new blooms can form from the same place. The *Hoya*'s peak flowering period falls during the summer months, when it can reward you with a really magnificent display.

These summer days are also ideal for taking cuttings of fuchsias, geraniums and other houseplants. Cut sideshoots and tip cuttings about 6–10cms long from fuchsias and geraniums, just below a bud or leaf node. Insert the cuttings carefully 2cms deep in a mixture of potting compost, peat fibre and river sand, or a ready-made proprietary cutting compost.

Cuttings of Oleander (*Nerium*), Passion Flower (*Passiflora*), Flame Nettle (*Coleus*), *Tradescantia*, Ivy (*Hedera*), Busy Lizzie (*Impatiens*) and *Begonia*, can be easily rooted in a bottle of water. The flowering *Rochea coccinia*, better known as *Crassula coccinia*, that bears clusters of carmine-red blooms, should be exposed to the morning sun, given lots of fresh air and not too much water. The Oleander (*Nerium*) should only be placed out of doors if you can provide it with a nice warm location, preferably against a south-facing wall. Succulents, such as the Carrion Flower (*Stapelia*), *Agave*, *Aloe*, *Haworthia* and *Gasteria* can also be cultivated outdoors during the summer, but take care not to expose them to too much direct sunlight. The Christmas or Winter Cherry (*Solanum*) that has been bedded in the garden in its pot now needs to be lifted a little and turned slightly every three weeks or so to prevent the roots from overdeveloping or reaching down into the garden soil through the drainage hole. Do not spray if the plant is in flower.

July

This holiday month poses special problems for the plant-lover. Your houseplants will certainly not survive any long absence if you do not take certain precautionary measures; advice is given elsewhere in this book under 'Plant Care During the Holidays'. Even if you are not leaving the house, your plants will, of course, need protection from the direct rays of the sun during this high summer month. They also need plenty of fresh air.

The Azalea will now be grateful for a daily spray, and most of your plants will be refreshed if placed under a gentle shower of rain at this time. The *Veltheimia* is now ready for its annual resting period; leave it to stand totally dry in its pot somewhere out of the way, and do not worry if the foliage dries up, as this is natural to the plant. Spraying with tapwater can often cause chalk marks to appear on the leaves, so use rainwater when you can, particularly for the Stag-horn Fern (*Platycerium*), bromelias, orchids and the Flame Nettle (*Coleus*). The Calla or Arum Lily (*Zantedeschia*) that is now emerging from its resting period should be given new, nourishing compost. It can be plunged outdoors, pot and all, if it is not exposed to too much sun. Covering the surface of the pot with a layer of peat fibre will help the plant to retain moisture. When new growth appears feed weekly with a nutrient solution, and spray when the weather is dry. The crown of the Christmas or Winter Cherry (*Solanum*), should not be sprayed once it has started into blossom. Gently brushing the flowers with a plume will encourage the buds to develop more profusely. This also applies to the Orange plant (*Citrus*). The House Lime or African Linden (*Sparmannia*) that has grown bare can be cut back to about 15cms above the soil. Tip cuttings and sideshoots about 10–20cms long, can be potted up in a mixture of leafmould and sharp sand. The House Lime may be plunged in the ground out of doors during the summer, in a sheltered, well-shaded spot, but make sure it will not be affected by dripping trees or shrubs. If you keep the plant indoors, give it an airy location near an open window in a cool room.

August

Large-flowered begonias should only be watered sparingly at this time of the year, and they are happiest in front of a window facing the morning or evening sun. There is little we can do with these plants once they have ceased flowering, but they are easily increased from cuttings.

The Bellflower (*Campanula isophylla*) now needs to be protected from the noonday sun; water moderately and feed weekly. This attractive plant comes into its own if the trailing stems are allowed to hang freely. Removing the withered blossoms each day will prolong flowering.

Cuttings can now be taken from the Piggyback Plant (*Tolmiea*). Detach a parent leaf with a tiny plantlet attached and place it (with a small section of stem) in a pot containing a mixture of leafmould and sharp sand.

The Amaryllis (*Hippeastrum*) should be allowed to rest this month if you wish it to bloom at Christmas.

The bulbs of the dry-flowering plant Meadow Saffron (*Colchicum*) can now be set up in a bowl or pot without soil, in front of a sunny window; shoots with flowers should appear within a few weeks.

The Oleander (*Nerium*) welcomes lots of sun, plenty of tepid water and regular feeding.

Gloxinia (*Sinningia*), *Streptocarpus*, African Violet (*Saintpaulia*), *Rechsteineria* (*Gesneria*) and *Crossandra*, however, must be protected from the sun.

Cuttings of geraniums and fuchsias, as described in June, will be even more successful if taken in this high summer month. This is also a good time for taking cuttings of African Violet (*Saintpaulia*). Select healthy stems about 2cms long, bearing a number of mature leaves, or eventually an entire stem, and insert them around the edge of a pot filled with peat fibre and sharp sand, or a proprietary cutting compost. Five or six leaf cuttings will give you the best chance of obtaining an attractive plant.

The *Ophiopogon* (Lily Turf), with green or white striped leaves, is a relatively unfamiliar houseplant. It bears clusters of white, not particularly attractive flowers, on short stalks. Later, however, beautiful green berries appear, that gradually turn dark blue. A cool room provides the best environment for this rather unusual plant, which should be sprayed regularly over the leaves during the summer.

September

Now is the time to order prepared bulbs for Christmas flowering. They can then be planted in good time at the beginning of October. Choose bulbs which are recommended for indoor cultivation.

The Amaryllis (*Hippeastrum*) can gradually be given less water now and feed should be withheld if you want to bring the plant into growth in December or January.

Azaleas that have been planted out in the garden should be potted up during this month, preferably in wide, rather shallow containers. They can then safely be left to stand outdoors for a few more weeks.

Bougainvillea and *Euphorbia pulcherrima* (Poinsettia), however, should now be brought indoors, as these are rather delicate plants. It is best to give them a sunny location in front of the window.

The Calla or Arum Lily (*Zantedeschia*) now needs to be watered freely, fed weekly and given lots of daylight in an airy, slightly heated location.

A *Veltheimia*, coming into growth after its dormant period, can now use a little more water. The plant likes a sunny location, and should not be repotted every year. If the surface soil has really dried out, replace it with some fresh compost.

If you still have any poinsettias and hydrangeas outdoors, it is wise to protect them from heavy rainfall with a plate of glass or clear plastic cover. The *Hydrangea* can eventually also be planted out without its pot in the garden, where it will grow as a robust shrub.

Cease feeding cacti now. The Christmas Cactus (*Zygocactus*), is also ready for its resting period; this means that the plant should be kept on the dry side in a not too cool room. The withered flowers of the Wax Plant (*Hoya carnosa*) should definitely not be removed: new buds can develop from the old ones. You can still take cuttings of houseplants until the second half of September; later on they will have less chance of developing good roots.

The *Aspidistra elatior* is a stouthearted plant that will do its level best to grow in the darkest and coldest spot in your home. The leaves of this Victorian veteran grow directly from the rootstock. If you give it a light position and a small but regular supply of fertiliser, the rootstock can bear flowers, which are called 'sitting flowers' as they have no stem.

Cuttings of garden plants that can be potted up and cultivated indoors to brighten our winter, are, among others: *Chrysanthemum*, Slipper or Purse Flower (*Calceolaria*), *Lantana* and *Felicia*. If you give them a heated location—thus depriving them of a rest period—they will give you a nice show of flowers in late autumn.

October

This is a good time for forcing Paperwhite *Narcissus*—daffodils; they need 4–6 weeks to come into flower.

The tulips and hyacinths you want to see brightening up the house at Christmas and the New Year should now be placed in bowls and pots. Unlike other bulbous plants, Paperwhites need not be stored in a cool, dark place.

The Poinsettia (*Euphorbia pulcherrima*), likes a spot in a warm room, with as much daylight as possible. Water freely and spray over the leaves; feed weekly.

All houseplants should, in fact, be given as light a location as possible, since their growth rate slows down during these shortening, darker days. This is natural, since the majority of plants now need to rest. However, a little more light is good for their general condition. An extra-lamp above their heads boosts the vigour of houseplants at this time, but guard against scorching.

Geraniums and fuchsias like a position in front of a sunny window in a cool, frost-free room. Likewise the Azalea; this rather sensitive plant does, however, need spraying daily over the crown with tepid water. And remember, it appreciates a weekly bath. Gradually reduce watering the Gloxinia (*Sinningia*) and the *Rechsteineria* (*Gesneria*); and discontinue feeding, since the foliage must be allowed to die off if it is to be kept for the following year.

The Amaryllis (*Hippeastrum*) can be put away dry in its pot in a moderately heated location.

When the *Ixora* has ceased flowering, give it a cooler location and 4–6 weeks' rest.

The *Primula obconica* should be repotted when it, too, has finished blooming; it is better not to pot this plant in a leafmould mixture, as this can cause yellowing of the leaves. A loam-based compost or a proprietary peat mix is best.

The *Camellia*, standing in a dry, warm room, should be sprayed on the buds each day. As soon as the buds have developed, leave the pot exactly where it is: do not move or even turn it.

Even though an *Achimenes* (Hot Water Plant) may sometimes appear to be totally dead, it should not be discarded, because the tuber-shaped rootstock can overwinter successfully in dry sand at 6–8°C. The plant can be repotted in lime-free compost in March.

The *Clivia* can now gladden the eye with a profusion of orange flowers. This plant likes a sunny location and a moderately warm temperature. It should not be given too much water, and can be allowed to remain almost dry from October on.

Watering should only be stepped up slightly when the flower-stalk is at least 15cms long. It then also needs a slightly warmer location.

Cacti and succulents now require a rest: cease watering and feeding. Garden herbs, such as chives, chervil, parsley and celery should now be brought indoors, before night-frost falls. They will almost certainly continue to grow if placed in suitable containers on a light, cool windowsill. Chervil and cress can still be sown successfully.

November

The House Lime or African Linden (*Sparmannia*) that is now developing buds should be placed in a cool room to prevent these newly formed buds from drying out. A sunny spot in front of the window is a good location for this attractive plant. It does, however, need some heat if the weather is freezing.

The Calla or Arum Lily (*Zantedeschia*), likewise needs a cool location; it does not tolerate a temperature above 16°C. Water freely; spray the leaves twice a week. The died-off Gloxinia (*Sinningia*), *Rechsteineria* (*Gesneria*) and *Achimenes* can be kept in their pots at a temperature of 6–8°C. Generally speaking, houseplants

should now be given less water and no fertiliser, as the growing process has now almost come to a standstill. During this period plants should definitely not be left standing in stagnant water; always check the drainage dishes soon after watering, as 'wet feet' can cause plants to pine away completely. This does not apply to flowering plants.

Given a well-lit situation, the African Violet (*Saintpaulia*) can go on blooming for a surprisingly long time. It should be 'misted' well above the leaves; moisten the atmosphere above the plant with the finest possible spray, since drops of water landing directly on the leaves can cause damage and leave ugly marks. Setting it on an 'island' of moist peat moss or wet pebbles also helps to create a little 'micro-climate'. The latter aids most plants living in centrally heated homes. When the Bellflower (*Campanula isophylla*) has finally finished blooming, cut it back to a few centimetres above the soil; ideally, it should be allowed to overwinter in front of a sunny window in an unheated room. Water sparingly and do not feed.

The budding Christmas Cactus (*Zygocactus*) needs a little more water now, but on no account move or turn the plant at this time.

The Amaryllis bulb (*Hippeastrum*) can be potted up towards the end of November, ready for Christmas flowering. Two-thirds of the bulb should remain visible above the soil; water sparingly for the first two weeks. It likes a warm position near a radiator, stove or fire.

Keep the *Sansevieria* and other succulents and cacti on the dry side now. The *Sansevieria* enjoys a temperature of 16°C.

A flowering *Erica gracilis* should be given a cool location and plenty of water.

Bromeliad-type plants in a centrally heated environment still need to be given tepid water through their funnel. However, once they have put forth flowers deep in the funnel or on a stem, watering should be done very carefully, as too much water at this time can cause rotting.

December

Bulbs that have been potted up in October can be brought into the warmth and light at the beginning of December. However, the flower buds

or the tops of the leaves should be 'nosing' about 6–8cms out of the bulb, so it is as well to check this. Ferns standing in the warm living room need a moist atmosphere; allow the water under the pot to evaporate, and spray frequently over the foliage. It also helps to place them in an outer container packed with damp peat moss, or another moisture-retaining substance. This also applies to *Anthurium*, *Peperomia*, *Fittonia*, *Maranta*, *Ruellia* and orchid species.

The foliage of the Poinsettia (*Euphorbia pulcherrima*) now appreciates a daily spray with tepid water, to prevent it dropping its beautiful red bracts and leaves.

The Wax Plant (*Hoya carnosa*) should overwinter at a temperature not below 12°C.

Budding azaleas can tolerate more warmth now, but continue spraying the leaf-crown until the buds start to colour.

The *Fatsia* (Japanese Aralia or 'false' Castor Oil Plant) requires a cool location; no water should be left standing in the drainage dish, otherwise it could drop its leaves. All plants should be given water that has been left standing in a warm room for at least 24 hours. Cultivate the habit of refilling the watering can as soon as it is empty, and leaving it in the same warmish place.

The leaf begonia (*Begonia Rex*) needs a warm position; do not be too generous when watering.

The budding *Camellia* now needs very careful treatment; it should no longer be turned with regard to the light, neither should the temperature be allowed to rise above 15°C. Water moderately and ensure that the roots do not dry out.

The Mother of Thousands (*Saxifraga stolonifera*) prefers a well-lit, cool room, with a minimum temperature of 10°C. This old-fashioned little plant needs a shallow pot in order to flourish at its best. The leaves are finely haired and light red on the underside. The thread-like runners bear completely new baby plantlets. These are often more attractive than the mother plant, so replacement by propagating them is often to be recommended. Watering sparingly in the winter can result in the plant bearing airy clusters of small, white flowers in the summer.

Plants in the home

Plants bring a breath of life into every interior, and create a cheerful 'lived-in' atmosphere in the home with their natural beauty. When choosing your indoor plants, it is wise to consider the conditions under which they will have to live. A sunny, south-facing windowsill, for example, offers different possibilities than a dark hall or a frequently damp bathroom. No matter how attractive a plant may look in a particular spot in the room, it will not flourish if it is not happy there. Another point is that your plants should harmonise with each other to some extent. Even the smallest vestibules, halls or work corners can be enlivened by a small foliage plant or a simple flower. The fact that plants can be placed in other areas than just the living room is, fortunately, being discovered and put into practice more and more nowadays.

Step inside...

The atmosphere of a house is not only determined by its living quarters: the reception area at the front door can also play a role. Vestibule, hall and stairway are the 'introducers' of every home. Here, visitors receive their first (or last) impression of you and yours, while the occupants themselves pass these portals daily with their comings and goings. Reason enough, you could say, to make these areas more welcoming and attractive. The smallest of hallways usually has some sort of window next to the front door, and this can well be decorated with suitable plants, even if it is merely to afford privacy. If the window reaches to the floor, the hall can be really brightened up by building a permanent cement trough on or in the ground just in front of it. Or you can place a narrow trough on the windowsill. If you plant the trough with fast-growing species such as *Cyperus* (Umbrella Plant), it will soon reward you with a beautiful screening curtain of greenery. However, not every windowsill is a suitable location for plants. Halls invariably lead to a number of doors, and the more doors, the more chance there is of draughts. And there is nothing plants abhor more than standing in a draught. So first check the positions of the doors in relation to one another. What happens when they are all open? If everything appears to be draught-free, you can start experimenting with some suitable plants. If after a while they produce a rich and vigorous growth, they can possibly be transferred from their separate pots into permanent, cement troughs. Keep the experiment going for a few seasons. Plants sometimes flourish in autumn and winter, but become sadly afflicted as spring approaches, because this is precisely when sudden heavy frosts can occur. The same hall will probably have a number of frost- and draught-free corners, but not in front of the window. Consider the possibility of trailing plants on the warm inside wall opposite the window, or on a cork memo-board, which not only provides space for notes, invitations, drawings and the like, but also acts as an attractive background for living greenery. And if your hall turns out to be too draughty for even the hardiest houseplants, it can still be brightened

Below: A hall with an open staircase is turned into a green indoor garden. Right: A homely memo-board gains added interest when framed with plants. Far right: A roomy hallway can really be enhanced by an imaginative plant combination, such as this cacti tub.

Overleaf: The happy possessor of a spacious hall or reception room can give full artistic expression to such a romantic corner with a profusion of various plants.

with dried flowers, in bunches on the ceiling or in artistically arranged bouquets. Dried hydrangeas, for instance, can look really splendid in an antique container.

Of course, the more spacious the entrance hall, the easier it is to turn it into a veritable haven of plants, especially as the amount of light coming in from the sides and roof is then relatively greater. A medium-sized hall, housing a telephone corner, with a table, chair or stool, can be greatly enhanced with a display of attractively grouped plants.

If little or no daylight reaches the hall, special plant-lights can provide an efficient alternative. Some houses have such a spacious, well-lit hall that the possibilities of creative plant displays are much greater. Then, easy chairs nestle among impressive, tree-like plants, or children play in the extra space under a cascade of greenery hanging from the daylight roof. Occasionally a wide hallway also provides enough space for a complete indoor greenhouse; the partition between living room and hall then consists of glass and tropical plants, that can be admired from all sides. This eloquent plant 'picture window' is, however, something of an exception. More usual, and more easily attainable, are the foliage-lined halls and stairways. These areas generally have at least one window which lets in daylight and sometimes sun.

Above: Even in a narrow hall it is still possible to brighten up a spot opposite a window with a suitable plant. Right: The corner of a landing, brilliantly bedecked with a colourful plant display.

Staircases and landings lend themselves well for plant decoration, particularly spiral or curving stairs. Climbing plants are particularly happy here; after all, they have plenty of supports to cling to! But keep the pruning knife handy and do not place any plantpots on the broadest tread of a stair, or you may be heading for a fall.

The *Rhoicissus rhomboide*, with its elegant leaves and brownish vines is a particularly fast and easy grower.

The creeping Ficus (*Ficus pumila* or *Ficus repens*) is likewise a fast-growing climber, with small, glossy leaves. Both species need a high degree of atmospheric humidity, so frequent misting with a fine spray is essential here. This is also necessary for the *Stephanotis floribunda* (Madagascar Jasmine) which, given the right conditions, can grow into a robust, trailing plant, with deliciously scented star-shaped flowers. If even the smallest amount of sun and daylight fails to penetrate the hall or stairway, then one or more plant-lights are an absolute necessity. There are various types of lamps available for different purposes. Moreover, some plants can tolerate relatively little light, others even prefer shadow or semi-twilight. Examples of such are the *Schefflera*, *Ficus elastica* (Rubber Plant), *Cissus*, *Sansevieria*, *Cyrtomium* (Holly Fern) and the green *Hedera*.

Above: A spiral staircase laced with a beautiful collection of plants. Left: This tropical indoor garden, with glass panelling sloping from roof to ground level, can be admired both from the side entrance and the living room.

Plants for the kitchen

When considering plants for the kitchen, the first things that spring to mind are herbs, and rightly so. No plant is more aromatic, and a supply of garden herbs within hands' reach is not only decorative but extremely useful. Not that it is particularly easy to grow a complete herb garden indoors. Their natural habitat is, of course, out in the fresh air and a large number of herb varieties are perennials, thus winter-hardy and not accustomed to warmth. They prefer to grow in the open ground and enjoy fresh, moist air. If the temperature in the kitchen proves to be too high for them, it is worth trying to grow your herbs in a flowerpot outdoors or planting them in the garden soil close to the kitchen door. However, if you wish to grow your herbs indoors, then the most convivial place for them is indeed the kitchen. Although this location is generally warmer than the plants prefer, evaporating liquids create an overall moist atmosphere here, which is something they also enjoy. If you spray frequently, open windows regularly and, weather permitting, place them under a gentle shower of rain each week, your windowsill could well become the fragrant focal-point of your kitchen. Herbs can now be bought at all kinds of different outlets. Some greengrocers, supermarkets and garden shops sell small pots of chives and thyme, flower shops and garden centres not only supply many different sorts of seed in specially prepared pots, but also packets of ordinary herb seed for direct sowing in containers or in the garden. As a result of their popular revival, the range of herbs is now so extensive that you don't have to look very far to find what you need.

Chives and thyme stand the best chance of survival on a sunny windowsill, as does marjoram, dill, basil and lemon melissa. If your chive plant fails to flourish indoors, placing it outside under a rose bush will work wonders. For chives and roses make very good companions; each encourages the other's vigour and bloom. Thyme can tolerate life indoors for a fairly long time if it is given a sunny position. Use the watering can very sparingly with this

Herbs and a scattering of easy-care ferns and hanging plants brighten both the view and the daily chores in the kitchen.

Above: A veritable orgy of greenery as soothing decor for a dining corner. Below: A group of extra-special plants . . . conversation pieces during mealtimes.

plant, but keep it moist by misting frequently with a fine spray. Parsley can flourish happily on a windowsill in the shade, likewise chervil, woodruff and celery. But on no account place parsley and celery next to each other. For some reason, these two plants simply cannot tolerate one another, and pairing them off invariably leads to their decline.

The kitchen is, of course, also an ideal place for 'ordinary' plants. Before choosing your plants, however, first consider the position of your kitchen in relation to the sun. As this is not usually the lightest room in the house, it is often best to choose a selection of shade-loving plants.

In a really spacious, kitchen-diner, plants grouped in large troughs can look really attractive. And if they are tall, you can possibly use the plant-troughs to screen off the kitchen work units, and in so doing place a great deal of chaos out of sight, if not out of mind! They can also function as a soothing, airy partition between the kitchen- and dining-area.

When planting the trough, try to select plants that look well together and have mutual needs as regards light, moisture and atmospheric humidity. It would be a great pity if, after a time, some specimens have to be removed from the trough because of their premature demise.

Your plants will not mind the rather high degree of atmospheric humidity in the kitchen in the least. On the contrary, they actually welcome it!

Dining among greenery

Numerous families also enjoy the presence of flowering plants and attractive foliage at mealtimes, even if this consists of nothing more than a 'simple flower' on the table. In fact, this is a feature of every type of home, be it a separate dining room of vast or tiny dimensions, a dining- or open-kitchen, or simply the corner of the living room or bedsitter. It is apparently a characteristic of human beings everywhere to want to sit down to eat in convivial, decorated surroundings . . . probably because this is a special sharing time, when the family comes together.

This convivial atmosphere can be created in many different ways. Those of us who have a really large dining table, with a surface greater than that needed for the place-settings, can extend the 'simple flower' idea into an entire group of decorative plants. But dining tables with less room for such

ambitious displays can also be turned into a special, cosy place at mealtimes, simply by the presence of a single flowering plant or attractive foliage.

To what extent other plants can be introduced here depends on the manner in which you and yours live and eat, the location of the dining area, and the amount of room available. The first point is a particularly relevant one in this respect. Occupants of old or completely renovated houses sometimes find themselves with a kitchen large enough to serve as the main room. This soon tends to become the hub of the house; children often do their home-work (and their crying!) here; there is room for the baby's playpen; and in some kitchens, space is even made for a piano. While such rooms can rarely be called the tidiest, they are, without doubt, the cosiest and most memorable place in the home.

Cooking is no lonely, isolated job in such houses; everyone can keep the cook company. There is room enough also for games and other pursuits. The windowsills and cupboard tops are usually festooned with plants in these kitchen-cum-living rooms, and there is also space near the dining table for an impressive group of plants in a trough.

These old-fashioned kitchens subsequently inspired architects to design the modern open kitchens. Although many housewives place great value on a kitchen door—when closed, it conveniently shuts out all cooking smells and kitchen chaos—others dislike being cut off in a separate room where they cannot follow the conversation going on in the living-room while preparing the food. And getting it to the table costs a lot of legwork! Many open kitchens are therefore equipped with a dining counter, that often acts as a cocktail bar or homework 'listening post'. When the work area in an open kitchen has space for only a narrow counter, there is usually a dining table in the adjoining room. With this arrangement the family generally use the

A 'living decor' of plants creates a friendly, relaxed atmosphere in every dining-room area.

kitchen counter for breakfast and light teas, while the dining table is laid for the main meal of the day.

When this table is situated near a window, it can be given a friendly green background with a decorative combination of plants. Mirrors can also often be used to good effect here. Not only the dining area, but many other places in the home, can appear to be twice as large with the subtle use of mirrors. But it is wise to be cautious here, since everything will be reflected, and if things are left lying around—toys, for instance—the chaos will also appear twice as much. It is perhaps a good idea to experiment with an (inexpensive) self-adhesive mirror on a door. If the effect is disappointing then the mirror can be easily removed without damage to any paintwork. If, on the other hand, it proves successful, then you can go ahead with more ambitious 'mirror-images', possibly covering entire walls. The self-sticking mirrors (which come in various types and sizes) are ideal for this purpose, or you could use reflecting foil or tiles, especially behind corner groups of plants, since the reflected light is beneficial to them. Most good do-it-yourself shops

Whether the dining table is in the kitchen or in a separate room, the surroundings are always enhanced by a decorative plant group, a single beautiful flower or an artistic arrangement of dried flowers.

will give advice, and those who want a really professional finish can, of course, have mirrors specially made to measure. In short, small rooms can be made to appear as large as you wish—it's all done with mirrors.

An elegant dining room, graced with a profusion of foliage plants, can be even more enhanced by this illusion of extra space.

Light from three sides

Not everyone given the choice between an old and new house will make the same decision. One person, without the slightest hesitation, will choose a modern house: after all, it is planned for efficiency, is easier to keep clean and it probably has central heating. Another will prefer an old house. The room arrangement is less predictable, it usually has lots of interesting nooks and crannies, and rooms which, with imagination and relatively little effort, can be turned into something really personal and special. Another plus-point with old houses is that they often have a conservatory adjoining the main living room. They consist largely of glass panels and serve as an airy portal between house and garden. Conservatories are specifically designed for the cultivation of plants under ideal conditions, although the glass panels should be hermetically sealed if the area is to be free of draughts. A great deal of rebuilding has been going on since the 1920's to make these rambling old houses warmer. But even in houses where the conservatory has disappeared, its former location is nearly always recognisable by a skylight.

The majority of plants are extremely happy with this type of overhead light —after all, this is primarily where it comes from in their natural environment. Plants will always turn towards the sunlight. This universal habit can be turned to advantage with plants living in the more diffused light of a house because they tend to crowd each other near a vertical window.

Overhead light is especially beneficial to epiphytes—plants that grow independently on other, larger species, without drawing nutrients from them. This is the natural habit of many orchid species that nestle in the crowns or between the branches of trees in the forests, sheltering under dense foliage where the light is always filtered. Moreover, many varieties of orchid grow in extremely humid regions. So whoever plans to grow these exotic flowers at home should be able to provide them with a permanently moist atmosphere, for they will definitely not be satisfied by sporadic misting with a fine spray.

Which other plants will be happy in the conservatory depends on its dimensions and on your own personal taste. Ferns make excellent ground plants, also under a glass roof. They flourish naturally as ground cover in the forests and woodlands.

If you intend to make full use of a conservatory, or even a modest lean-to with a skylight, it is essential to provide it with good sun-screens, as the heat of the noonday sun is too much of a good thing for the majority of plants. One really attractive solution is to train climbing plants up the outside of the glass. However, not all species are suitable for this purpose, since it is necessary that they drop their leaves in winter. During this season plants in our climate have more need of sunlight than of sun-screens.

Below left: Cane and rattan furniture is both decorative and practical in a conservatory filled with plants that need a high degree of atmospheric humidity. Below centre: Lots of light, air and space—a truly ideal plant situation; here they can be sprayed to the heart's content. Below right: A flourishing winter garden lit by skylights; also suitable for the cultivation of orchids. Far right: The luxuriant greenery in this cosy corner of a conservatory enjoys light from both side windows and roof.

Working among greenery

The first 'office gardens' began to appear in a number of European countries towards the end of the 60's: spacious, open workrooms that are no longer split up into small cubicles, where the staff have their own place in the same large area. Of course, individual privacy must also be catered for, even if it is only to prevent people from being distracted by the general buzz of activity. A well-designed office garden is therefore usually equipped with special, noise-reducing, thick floor covering, insulated ceilings, sometimes soft background music, and a large number of plant-troughs and tubs. In fact, it was this 'sea of greenery' that gave such locations their name.

The presence of plants during working hours proved to be a resounding success; other offices and factories soon took up this 'horticultural habit'. And nowadays there are very few workrooms and offices that have neither the place nor the money for plants. The use of plants is also often taken into account when a company renovates or extends its building.

Not every plant, however, is suitable for life in an office or workshop. Even

Below: The first heralds of spring enjoy pride of place on a desk in a work corner. Right: Peacefully working among soothing greenery in the little work-room in the attic.

before making a choice, hardly anyone bothers to ask the staff whether there is anybody with green fingers who would be willing to take on the daily job of caring for all the plants. And if a plant-loving volunteer does step forward, this is no guarantee that the office greenery will flourish indefinitely, since not everyone remains in the same job all his life and people retire sooner or later. For this and other reasons, it is best to select the most hardy veterans of the plant world, who have proved their capacity for endurance and do not make strict demands as regards atmospheric humidity, warmth and light.

With a sensible basic selection, one can create a veritable 'landscape' of plants that make a working environment very much more agreeable. Under ideal circumstances (plant-lovers on the staff?) the stock of plants is increased, with young plants propagated at home. Unfortunately, such is not the happy lot of every office, but when it is, the office garden can really become a veritable Garden of Eden! Without careful tending it would, in any case, be impossible to bring cuttings into vigorous growth in an office which is, moreover, usually empty at weekends. This is why many companies are now using special cultivating methods, such as hydroponics, water retaining devices and moisture meters, which indicate, by colour, how much water a plant still has available. Occasionally a florist is employed on a regular basis to care for the many troughs and tubs. Although there are many people who lack even a single green finger, they certainly appreciate a green working environment.

A private workroom or work corner is, of course, a lot easier to decorate with plants than a strictly functional office. At home you only have the location, furnishing and your own taste to consider. Choice sometimes falls on a less austere desk, often accompanied by a not so functional chair—and the decorations are more personal. A private retreat at home such as this can be made even more welcoming with an attractive display of plants. Living greenery softens the business-like effect and makes working at home a pleasant occupation.

Of course, work corners, workrooms and studies are different in every house, so it is important to choose the right plants for the right surroundings. Sometimes, for the sake of peace and quiet, a workroom is isolated from the rest of the house, and plants in such a location are unlikely to be tended every day. It is therefore best to select only undemanding, sturdy plants, such as the *Yucca* family. The nearer the workroom is to the rest of the house, the greater the choice of plants becomes—in this case, the occupants are not as likely to be distracted by someone walking in with a watering-can. The work corner in a living room can be really cheered up by a living green decor. Large plants placed between this corner and the rest of the room can also function as a subtle, but friendly partition. The number and arrangement of the plants in the work corner itself depends largely on the person who will be using it most. There are those who really appreciate it if the first bowl of flowering bulbs is given a place of honour on their desk, while others may consider this an intrusion of their 'inner sanctuary'—then plants are best kept out of the way. But whatever plants you choose, make sure they receive careful attention. Nobody likes to find fallen leaves and spilled water among the papers on 'their' desk.

Top: Plants are invariably well looked after in work corners like this one.
Above: Work is pleasant in a large open-plan office, with the quiet companionship of well cared for plants.
Left: Even in this strictly functional, smaller office, the cool business-like atmosphere is softened by a few sizeable plant-troughs.

Good companions

Whoever plants a plant-trough for the first time can approach the task in two ways. With the first method, all the plants remain in their own clay pot, and are placed next to each other in a trough filled with peat-fibre, which should be kept well moistened at all times. The second method is to fill the trough with an appropriate nourishing compost and plant the plants directly in this, without their pots. In troughs without drainage holes, it is absolutely essential to place a substantial layer of crocks (broken pieces of clay pots) at the bottom.

The first method is generally the safest. If the display turns out to be something of a disappointment, because of unsuitable grouping, for example, all is not lost—you can simply rearrange the pots. If you are using newly-bought plants for your trough, it is important to check the roots as well as the pots. Growers are inclined to keep plants in rather small pots to encourage a compact root-ball. So there is a good chance that the plants will need repotting into slightly larger containers as soon as you have bought them. Plants in plastic pots should be transferred into terracotta clay pots, as these are the only ones porous enough to absorb the moisture necessary for the root-ball from the surrounding peat-fibre. If you are already familiar with plant-troughs and are satisfied with the new selection of plants, then you can follow the second method. Tap the plants carefully from their pots and plant them directly, in a harmonious group, in a trough filled with appropriate compost. A collection of houseplants grouped together like this gives a more natural effect and encourages vigorous growth.

Grouping plants in troughs according to 'colour' is fascinating and extremely rewarding work, but it does require some experience. Moreover, the various species selected for the same trough must also have mutual cultivation needs. One charming, blue-flowering combination, for example, is made up of *Jacaranda mimosifolia*, *Plumbago auriculata*, *Streptocarpus* and *Fittonia verschaffeltii argyroneura*.

All these plants require about 5 hours' sunlight each day and a normal supply of water. All kinds of harmonious combinations—even in brown or pink—can be created in this way by a plant-lover with basic experience. Rather surprisingly, it is also possible to plant a luxuriant trough in front of a north-facing window, which hardly receives any sunlight. The tall *Dracaena marginata* and the smaller *Dracaena godseffiana* with its succulent-like, spotted leaves, make a particularly handsome couple. Various fern species, such as the Shield Fern (*Polystichum falcatum*) and the Roundleaf or Button Fern (*Pellaea rotundifolia*), are also hardy and enduring inhabitants of a north-facing plant-trough.

The requirements of those other good companions, the cacti and the succulents, are lots of sun and little water.

If you wish to combine a number of plants with differing cultivation requirements, they can be placed in separate containers, possibly of varying sizes but made of the same material, such as acid- or fish-tanks, or square tubs. It is also helpful to place really large containers on castors.

Above: A luxuriant ornamental container with tall dracaenas rising impressively above an arrangement of ferns and succulents. Far right: A carefully chosen collection of 'blues' as described above. Opposite page: Separated in their own acid tanks, these grouped plants can still receive the particular individual care they need.

Bedroom greenery

In former times plants were never to be found in bedrooms. As the name suggests, this room was once strictly for sleeping in. The floor was invariably covered with cold linoleum, on which stood the bedroom suite and perhaps a marble washstand, complete with porcelain bowl and jug, and possibly a single chair on which to hang clothes. This more or less completed the picture of the traditional bedroom. It was hygienic, strictly functional and easy to keep clean, and that was about it. In sharp contrast to other rooms in the house, anything that could gather dust was considered taboo in a bedroom—vacuum cleaners were still something of a luxury— and massive doses of oxygen were regarded as vital to everyone's health. Consequently: no plants in the bedroom!

Although living plants release plenty of oxygen under the influence of light,

Above left: Plants have their own spacious setting in this raised-platform bedroom. Above: This small, light, side-bedroom is an excellent retreat for plants. Right: A small workroom with a bunk-bed still has space over for some decorative foliage.

they cannot survive without it in the dark. But providing you position them sensibly and keep the room fresh and well ventilated, there is no reason why they, too, cannot spend the nights there.

Modern houses are beneficial for plants in other respects, too. When central heating was still a rarity, plants could easily freeze during ice-cold winter nights, while their owners snuggled under thick blankets. But in today's centrally-heated homes the temperature in the bedroom is seldom Siberian, and even when the radiator is turned off, the warm pipes take the worst chill off. Consequently bedrooms are now often graced with a profusion of vigorous flowering and foliage plants that really enjoy the somewhat cooler environment. The species of plants that will flourish best here largely depends on the situation of the house. North- or east-facing rooms afford other possibilities than those on the south or west side. The amount of sun and light entering the rooms should also be taken into account when making a final choice.

Totally unsuitable for this environment are plants that originally came from tropical or sub-tropical regions and thus require a more or less constant temperature of 20°C or higher. Other plants, however, flourish exceptionally well here. There are people who can only keep cyclamens looking their best on the cool windowsill of a bedroom. Azaleas can also sometimes be encouraged to flower again much earlier in this cooler location. One of the most companionable of bedroom plants is undoubtedly the House Lime or African Linden (*Sparmannia*) which has the charming habit of turning into a beautiful blossoming tree in the coldest season of the year, when clusters of white flowers appear among the large, light-green leaves between January and April. The same House Lime appreciates being given a place in the garden during the summer, in a sheltered spot with plenty of nourishing soil. There are also plants that will not thank you for warmth in the winter but like to be protected from frost. It is not always easy to find a suitable spot for them during the winter in our modern, warm houses—even garages and larders are often too warm. In view of this, bedrooms have been found to function as useful alternatives to the conservatories of days gone by. With daylight, plant-lights and just enough warmth for a frost-free environment,

Above: Even a House Lime or another large shrub-like plant flourishes very well in a bedroom. Below: Ferns are also equally happy in this same location. Left: Light-a-plenty for plants in this spacious, modern bedroom.

there are numerous species of plants that will gladly overwinter there. And is there not something alluring about sleeping amid a winter garden?
If you keep your troughs or tubs of geraniums here, they need only to be pruned back in the spring before you place them outdoors again. Bulbs can also benefit from a bedroom environment, when they are not quite ready for the warmth of the living room. The costly Bay Tree and *Buxus* shrub seldom survive a winter of constant warmth and dry air. The *Buxus* is really a winter-hard species in origin. After all, it has been carefully cultivated for centuries as an exceptional pruned shrub or tree; it can therefore be safely moved out onto a balcony or patio—with pleasure, in fact! But if this is not possible, the next best place in winter is a cool bedroom with a high degree of atmospheric humidity.

The Bay Tree is somewhat less tolerant of the cold, but it, too, abhors a warm living room. This plant actually feels most comfortable during the winter at a temperature of 1–6°C. The arrangement of plants in bedrooms is, of course, different in every house. Perhaps there is a broad windowsill or a small table in front of the window; use can be made of an unused fireplace or an alcove; and in some ultra-modern bedrooms a platform bed area may include a built-in plant-trough. There is also nothing against broadening a windowsill, particularly in a bay window, or turning an old window-seat into a plant container. When extending a sill, remember to leave a gap or place a grid in it, if there is a radiator underneath. The warm air must be able to rise up—behind the plants but in front of the window pane. Otherwise there is a risk of them freezing to the glass on bitterly cold nights, and this is certainly not your intention, or that of the plants.

Bathing in nature

Tropical plants do not feel particularly at home with us, and no wonder. There is a world of difference: growing up in the filtered light under a dense canopy of tall trees in a humid tropical rainforest—or in a pot on the windowsill, above a radiator. Our struggling little pots of *Bougainvillea*, for instance, can in no way compare with the tumbling luxuriance of their kind on the flower-laden walls of southern France. Even the *Ficus* plants, that with tender care can grow into impressive shrubs, are mere pygmies compared to the great, towering specimens that grow wild in a country such as Brazil. Yet there is one place in our houses where tropical plants can feel more at home: the bathroom.

When this room is heated, and frequent use is made of the shower and/or bath, it creates the sort of humid atmosphere which comes closer to that prevailing in the tropical forests. The more a family baths, the happier are the tropical plants. Since they are regularly moisturised by their human 'bath-mates', there is no need for the plant caretaker to go around the house with the spray.

Tropical plants feel very much at home in the moist, warm atmosphere of a bathroom. Even in a small bathroom it is possible to find a suitable place for a few shade-loving plants.

Much as we enjoy having tropical plants in our regions, we cannot offer them a natural environment, but a warm, humid bathroom serves as a fair imitation. It is an ideal location for ferns and species of *Monstera* (Swiss Cheese Plant) that clamber up the forest giants in their native habitat. If a bathroom is equipped with a skylight or other overhead lighting, it is even possible to cultivate orchids.

But no matter how well adapted temperature and humidity may be, no plants can survive without light. Tropical plants are no lovers of direct sunlight—they are, after all, well adjusted to filtered light in their native habitat. A north-facing window comes fairly close to this, but from whatever direction the light may enter, one can always guard against too much sun. If the bathroom has no windows, lamps can also work wonders. When fitting lights, however, remember that there are special safety rules for 'wet locations', also specially adapted light-bulbs and electric fittings.

One possible idea would be to decorate the bathroom exclusively with tropical marsh- and water-plants. These are unlikely to come to an untimely end in such a compatible environment, since they flourish in saturated ground.

If the idea of 'bathing among the marshlands' appeals to you, it is best to start off with glass acid- or fish-tanks. If space allows, you could build a special trough for these plants—possibly using the same tiles as those of the bathroom.

Open-plan living

One seldom needs to view a house from the cellar to the roof in order to work out roughly when it was built. The architectural period can often be gathered from the structural design or from interior details, such as the arrangement of the rooms. No matter how much renovation takes place over the years, the basic structure of a house seldom loses its identity. Before the Second World War houses were traditionally equipped with a suite of rooms—demurely modest or spaciously grand, the arrangement was basically the same. One room served as dining room, the other as 'parlour', 'lounge' or 'front room', and these two rooms were invariably separated either by a wall or a sliding door. Every self-respecting family strove to keep the 'front room' serenely spotless for special occasions, and did most of their dining, and living, in the other room.

But this tradition, along with so many others, changed radically after the Second World War. In those days, architects, contractors and the future occupants of new houses were unanimous in their preference, if not in their reasons, for open-plan interiors. Young families found a suite of rooms linked by doors and corridors impractical and old-fashioned. They preferred one large, efficient living room which let in daylight from at least two sides. Thus came about the rapid rise of countless open-plan flats and family houses; the landscape was soon peppered with vast estates. And no wonder!

The 'green curtain' of plants, contrasting in height and foliage, looks particularly attractive in front of the large window in this flat.

The housing problem was so great that pressing on with more and more buildings was considered a higher priority than research into other possibilities. These had to wait until the most urgent housing needs had been met. Open-plan houses and flats have many agreeable features, which continually move with the times. Though it is argued that, in comparison with old houses, more imaginative flair is called for to give them a personal identity. In the average open-plan house, the dining area is situated next to the kitchen (where there is often a serving hatch), with the rest of the room functioning as a lounge; it would be impractical to situate the dining area further down the room.

These open dining-cum-living rooms are not only pleasing places for people to live in, they are also an excellent environment for plants. The changing light, coming in from large picture windows, usually at each end of the room, is more than enough to satisfy the needs of most houseplants. Even people who are 'absolutely hopeless with plants' can create beautiful flower and green foliage arrangements in front of these windows. Various plants are sometimes grouped together in special plant-tables or large cubes; elsewhere built-in or loose troughs are used to great effect, and occasionally a sizeable section of the floor is raised to form seating and accommodate sunken plant-troughs. This last innovation can make such an interior exceptionally cosy and welcoming.

It is, however, more difficult to grow plants in the middle of an open-plan interior. The strength of the incoming light, as far as plants are concerned, drops dramatically if they are placed more than one metre away from the light source. This can be a bit of a problem, since some sort of visual break is often just what these long rooms need; moreover, many people like to create an intimate corner by separating the living and dining area with a screen of plants. It is possible, however, even in the relatively darker centre of the room, if you use shade-loving plants. Look around a good garden centre and select the plants you find most attractive, but do seek advice about their upkeep, and you will find detailed descriptions of many suitable species at the back of this book. Finally, plant-lights can serve you and your plants really well in a dark spot, and investing in these lighting aids will also immediately increase the possibilities of arranging your plants.

Above: An open-plan living room composed entirely of a raised platform surrounding a sunken lounge area. Bottom left: A cemented brick-trough filled with green and variegated foliage makes an attractive break in a long, narrow room. Below: A serene plant corner and, on the radiator, cactus plants that happily tolerate the dry, warm air.

Living decor

Every interior can be enhanced with plants. Depending on choice and arrangement, they can also be either stimulating or soothing. This is true not only for office gardens, workshops, showrooms and ultra-modern interiors, filled with chrome and lacquered walls, but also a restored historical mansion, complete with baroque furnishings. When one sees how naturally flowers and plants complement and blend with such dramatically different decors, one realises just how timeless nature is. Fortunately nobody has ever introduced a fashion in which there is no place for 'living' decor. There are, of course, periodic fashions in plants, but these, related to particular species. At one time, for instance, nearly every home boasted a giant House Lime or African Linden, but this eventually disappeared from the 'limelight' for years, while it is now clearly making a successful comeback. There are no fixed rules for the choice of plants in any particular interior—this is essentially a matter of taste and the measure with which the plant-lover has been blessed with 'green fingers'.

Left: Even a room exclusively furnished in Art Deco style radiates more warmth through the friendly presence of 'living decor'. Above: A charming display of hydrangeas grouped harmoniously with ornamental objects. Above and below right: The atmosphere of every interior becomes much cosier with an arrangement of suitable flowering or foliage plants.

*Above: Shady nook for a kitten.
Left: This stall in a renovated
farmhouse has been transformed into
spacious, elegant living quarters,
suitable for large groups of plants.*

*Left: This beautiful arrangement of
hydrangeas is delicately complemented
by just a few attractive pieces of
pottery. Far right and overleaf: A
grandly spacious living room in a
renovated farmhouse with sculptured
furnishings and other artistic
decorations, amongst a veritable forest
of luxuriant plumbagos and chestnut
vines.*

Certainly, the contemporary furnishings in many modern homes are often
accentuated by the robust, spiny *Yucca*, but these exotic plants are equally
popular in older houses. No wonder! This extended plant-family (40 species)
actually flourishes if it is allowed to dry out completely from time to time;
it responds better to a certain amount of neglect than to a daily supply of
water. Modern houses are further often graced with various *Dracaena*
species, particularly the long-lasting *D. fragrans massangeana*. The wave of
nostalgia that seems to be lapping over the younger generation recently, has
also reawakened a lively interest in other 'old-fashioned' plants. The
Hydrangea, Kentia Palm and *Clivia*—those former sentinels of the Victorian parlour, tea-shop and reception hall—are once more on view, but this
time in the most trendy modern interiors.

Green foliage in particular is now being used in a more light-hearted
fashion: 'old' and 'new' plants can be tastefully combined in a room with
black lacquered panelling and chrome-steel fittings. When they are grouped
'companionably' together in a large trough, plants can create the same
harmonious effects as that between modern and antique furniture, or old
schoolroom prints in an ultra-modern setting.

Other houses are carefully and exclusively furnished to reflect a certain period style—such as the Art Nouveau round the turn of the century, or the Art Deco period which followed it in the Twenties. Plants, however, are indispensable even in such sophisticated surroundings, since they greatly improve the atmosphere wherever they are. And if they are left out, no matter how beautiful the decor, the overall impression is likely to be that of a rather lifeless showroom. Yet some restraint is necessary, too, as it would be a pity to clutter up a carefully assembled interior with too many different species of plants; better to keep to a few well-selected varieties. Kentia Palms, for instance, combine beautifully with the silver and grey tints of Art Deco. But this is a very personal matter, and if other plants are preferred, then they should certainly be used. After all, free expression is as rewarding with plants as it is with most other creative occupations.

Rattan, bamboo and split-cane are being seen in more and more homes nowadays. These reasonably inexpensive materials, which are lightweight and very versatile, are evidently also enjoying a popular revival. Rattan and wood go exceptionally well together. Long bamboo or rattan canes, split down the middle, make attractive trimmings to any number of objects; they

Below: All the furnishings of this interior, up to the tiles on the ceiling, are made of cane and rattan. The exotic atmosphere is further emphasised by beautifully arranged plant groups which include some unusual species.

can even decorate ceilings when treated with transparent lacquer and glued onto plain wood panelling. Split-cane, rattan or bamboo furniture, basketry work and rush matting, give a room an exotic, tropical atmosphere, that can be doubly emphasised with suitable plants, such as ferns and palms.

Those of us lucky enough to live in old farmhouses or renovated barns have much greater opportunities for placing and hanging plants. A former cow-shed or stable that has been turned into living quarters offers ample space for those robust shrubs and great green cascades, that would practically fill a room in the 'ordinary' house. City dwellers sometimes despair when their modest plants grow into towering shrubs, but these giants really come into their own in a spacious location. There is surely a good opportunity for a nice plant-exchange trade here.

Displaying plants in groups

A much more attractive arrangement in a long, fairly narrow room is to display your plants in two or three groups, in place of numerous separate specimens. Plant combinations concentrated in two or three good places are far more effective than small spots of greenery dotted all over the room. This is not only true for the open-plan living room, but for the entire house. It is also a good basic rule, even if you have only a handful of plants. Not only do plants benefit by this close proximity, but the decorative effect is immediately heightened when they are combined in an attractive display. They are also relatively easier to care for combined in this way, particularly when spraying, and seem more at home that when they are lined up like soldiers along the windowsill. Neither need the combination consist entirely of plants. An arrangement is often enhanced, and personalised, if other decorative accessories are added—a cherished piece of sculpture, a figurine, a wooden carving, candlesticks, decorative gourds, painted stones, driftwood . . . whatever you have to hand or may come across. You can even reverse the process, and arrange your plants around a favourite object. A group of 'living stone' plants and cacti, for instance, look splendid perched on the ridges of a large, uneven rock.

Top: This small table has an air of quiet intimacy, with its arrangement of simple foliage and blooms. Above: The somewhat monotonous brick wall gains considerably in interest with the addition of some decorative elements and a display of graceful plants.

Right: Palm species, such as this impressive Date Palm—incidentally, a fairly costly investment—generally require a rather warm location.

Right: A colourful collection of flowering plants—cheering companions at tea-time.

Above: African Violets not only look prettier but also appreciate such an extra light source, particularly in the winter.

An open-fronted china cabinet can be given a finishing touch with plants. In some homes one occasionally sees an open cupboard or shelf unit painted in a pastel colour (pale pink, blue or green), containing ceramics and other ornamental objects, which complement this basic tint. When green plants are added to such a background, the overall effect becomes even more attractive.

Occasionally a plant-placing problem can be solved by positioning a couple of wooden benches in front of the window; one serves for short coffee breaks and the other as a permanent spot for your plants.

Widening the windowsill

Although windowsills are an ideal place for single plants, they are not generally suitable for displaying plant groups. Their measurements were not designed for such a purpose, certainly not in newly-built houses. However, something can be done about this, and it need not necessarily be a complex job. It is often fairly easy to fix a wider plank on top of the existing sill. If you plan to make the sill really wide, it will need supporting brackets underneath; a collapsed plank could have dire consequences! When choosing the wood, or other material, for this job, remember to take into account the amount of weight it will have to carry—especially on the extending edge: your dealer will probably be happy to advise you on this subject.

Right: A beautifully flowering old-fashioned Clivia. Far right: With a little imagination you can create a charming windowsill for a sizeable group of small plants.
Opposite page: Children can really act out their 'make-believe' games under such a mantle of palm leaves, in this spacious room.

In a roomy, tastefully furnished interior, groups of plants, plant-troughs and fresh flowers blend harmoniously with the dried flower arrangements on top of the cupboards.

If you widen the windowsill in a centrally-heated house, it will probably extend over the radiator. In which case, the plank needs to be fitted with some sort of grille or slats—the warm air should be able to rise freely, preferably behind the plants.

Alternatively, if you wish to widen the windowsill without resorting to carpentry, a couple of tables the same height as the sill can also be effective here; if necessary, you could use blocks to raise them to the right level. Half-moon hall tables may prove useful for this. When your plants are harmoniously grouped on these tables in front of the window, the effect is really rewarding. Houses with floor heating also provide good opportunities for displaying plant combinations. The convector grids are often situated in the floor under the window, and in such houses the extended windowsill can be deeply scallop-shaped. This attractive, and useful, scalloped edge can also be achieved by using console tables, or legged tables wide enough to reach over the grids.

Right and far right: A couple of old favourites from grandmother's time: a Cape Primrose and an Azalea. Opposite page: A combination of tall-growing plants make a filtered, airy green screen in front of the window, and there is no nicer way of ensuring your privacy!

Abutilon
Indian Mallow, Flowering Maple or
Chinese Lantern

Flowering: summer and autumn.
Situation: light, airy, preferably out
of doors in summer.
Care: water freely during flowering
and feed fortnightly; reduce watering
in October.
Humidity: high.
Temperature: 10–12°C in winter.
Repotting: every spring.
Compost: leafmould, loam and rotted
cow manure.
Propagation: cuttings, from seed.

Acacia
Mimosa, Golden Wattle

Flowering: spring.
Situation: light, cool, possible
outdoors in summer.
Care: syringe with tepid water, feed
fortnightly in spring and summer.
Humidity: high.
Temperature: 6–8°C in winter.
Repotting: after flowering.
Compost: pinewood soil or
leafmould, rotted cow manure, sharp
sand with clay-loam.
Propagation: cuttings, from seed.

Acalypha
Beefsteak Plant, Chenille Plant,
Foxtails or Red Hot Cat's Tail.

Flowering: spring, autumn.
Situation: very light, warm, no direct
sunlight.
Care: keep well moist (on a water
island), syringe frequently and feed
fortnightly.
Humidity: high.
Temperature: 16–18°C.
Repotting: spring, if necessary.
Compost: leafmould with rotted cow
manure and sharp sand or loam.
Propagation: cuttings.

Achimenes
Cupid's Bower or Hot Water Plant

Flowering: summer.
Situation: warm, light, no sunlight.
Care: keep moist, provide humid
atmosphere (on an 'island'), give tepid
water during flowering, feed every
two weeks; keep dry during winter.
Humidity: high.
Temperature: 8°C during winter.
Repotting: every spring.
Compost: light and airy, leafmould,
peat fibre with rotted cow manure.
Propagation: from tuberous
rootstock (rhizome) from cuttings.

Adiantum
Maidenhair Fern

Flowering: none.
Situation: light, no direct sunlight.
Care: keep well moist, particularly
surrounding atmosphere.
Humidity: high.
Temperature: 16–20°C.
Repotting: in early spring.
Compost: leafmould, rotted cow
manure and peat fibre.
Propagation: by division.

Aechmea
Air-Pine or Coral Berry

Flowering: spring–autumn.
Situation: light, no direct sunlight.
Care: water freely, also in the funnel
when not in flower; feed every two
weeks.
Humidity: high.
Temperature: 15–18°C.
Repotting: do not repot.
Compost: peat-moss and well-rotted
beech leafmould, sharp sand, rotted
cow manure.
Propagation: from sideshoots,
produced when original rosette dies
off.

Aeonium
House Leek Tree

Flowering: spring.
Situation: sunny, cool in winter.
Care: water moderately, very
sparingly during resting period.
Humidity: low.
Temperature: not under 10°C.
Repotting: when new growth appears.
Compost: leafmould and clay-loam.
Propagation: leaf cuttings, from seed,
by offsets in spring.

Aeschynanthus
Basket Vine or Lipstick Vine

Flowering: summer.
Situation: light, no sun.
Care: water freely with rainwater,
syringe frequently, feed every two
weeks.
Humidity: very high.
Temperature: at least 18°C.
Repotting: very rarely.
Compost: proprietary potting
compost, peat moss and rotted cow
manure.
Propagation: from cuttings of stem
tips or sections.

Agave
Century Plant

Flowering: seldom, usually only after
10 years or more.
Situation: sunny.
Care: water only during the summer,
keep cool and dry during the winter.
Humidity: low.
Temperature: minimum frost-free.
Repotting: in spring.
Compost: leafmould, clay-loam and
sharp sand.
Propagation: sideshoot cuttings and
from seed.

Aglaonema
Chinese Evergreen

Flowering: seldom.
Situation: light, no direct sunlight.
Care: spray frequently with tepid
rainwater, feed every two weeks.
Humidity: very high.
Temperature: approximately 20°C.
Repotting: every spring.
Compost: loam-based compost or a
peat mix.
Propagation: cuttings, by division.

Allamanda
Golden Trumpet

Flowering: spring.
Situation: sunny; screen from direct
noonday sun in the summer.
Care: spray frequently and water
with tepid rainwater; feed
fortnightly, except during dormant
period.
Humidity: high.
Temperature: 18°C minimum.
Repotting: into a larger pot in the
spring.
Compost: fine loamy clay, rotted
cow manure and leafmould.
Propagation: from stem cuttings in
spring and summer.

Aloe
Tree Aloe

Flowering: varies according to
species.
Situation: light, sunny, screen from
hottest sun during summer.
Care: keep moist and feed regularly
during growing period; water more
sparingly in winter.
Humidity: low.
Temperature: cool, frost-free during
resting period.
Compost: clay-loam and leafmould.
Repotting: when necessary.
Propagation: offset cuttings.

Ampelopsis
Virginia Creeper

Flowering: none.
Situation: light, screen from direct sunlight.
Care: keep compost moist, feed fortnightly during growth; keep cool and dry during winter resting period.
Humidity: moderate.
Temperature: 10°C minimum.
Repotting: in spring.
Compost: garden soil, leafmould, rotted cow manure and sharp sand.
Propagation: cuttings, in peat fibre and sharp sand.

Ananas
Pineapple

Flowering: rarely.
Situation: sunny.
Care: keep nicely moistened, water with rainwater if possible, also in the funnel.
Humidity: high.
Temperature: 18–22°C.
Repotting: when necessary.
Compost: leafmould, rotted cow manure and peat fibre (sphagnum moss).
Propagation: remove leafy rosette from the top of the fruit and let it root under plastic.

Anthurium
Flamingo Flower

Flowering: spring–autumn.
Situation: light, screen from direct sunlight.
Care: water freely, sponge leaves weekly with tepid rainwater; feed once a fortnight.
Humidity: high.
Temperature: not lower then 15°C.
Repotting: after flowering.
Compost: special anthurium soil or leafmould with sphagnum moss and rotted cow manure.
Propagation: by division.

Aphelandra
Zebra Plant, Saffron Spike or Tiger Plant

Flowering: spring–summer.
Situation: light, no direct sunlight.
Care: water and spray freely, feed fortnightly, cut off blooms after flowering; water more sparingly during resting period, then cut back.
Humidity: high (ensure moist air by setting plant on an 'island' surrounded by water).
Temperature: 18–25°C.
Repotting: after resting period.
Compost: leafmould, rotted cow manure and rotted turves; or a proprietary peat mix.
Propagation: cuttings under plastic.

Araucaria
Norfolk Island Pine

Flowering: none.
Situation: light, cool, no sun.
Care: water freely during the summer and feed fortnightly; water sparingly in winter.
Humidity: low.
Temperature: minimum frost-free.
Repotting: spring.
Compost: 2 parts woodland soil to 1 part leafmould; rotted cow manure, some sharp sand; or a proprietary peat mix.
Propagation: from seed, or possibly from tip-cuttings.

Ardisia
Coral Berry

Flowering: April–May.
Situation: light, screen from direct sunlight.
Care: water freely in autumn, spray regularly, but not during flowering; feed every two weeks.
Humidity: fairly high.
Temperature: 10–16°C.
Repotting: when necessary.
Compost: proprietary peat mix with sharp sand.
Propagation: from seed (sow seed from ripe berries in peat fibre with sharp sand), or by lateral shoots taken as cuttings.

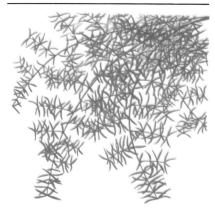

Asparagus
Asparagus Fern, Plume Asparagus or
Foxtail Asparagus

Flowering: summer.
Situation: little to moderate light,
shade from the sun in summer.
Care: water fairly freely in summer,
feed fortnightly; reduce watering in
winter and keep in a cooler location.
Humidity: fairly high.
Temperature: minimum of 10–15°C.
Repotting: spring.
Compost: leafmould, rotted cow
manure, some sharp sand; or loam-
based compost.
Propagation: by division or from
seed.

Aspidistra
Bar-room Plant, Cannonball Plant
or Cast Iron Plant

Flowering: not significant, produces
stalkless flowers at soil level.
Situation: little to moderate light is
sufficient, no sunlight.
Care: no special attention is needed;
the variegated leaf species 'Variegata'
requires more light, but less
nutritious soil.
Humidity: moderate.
Temperature: moderately warm to
cool.
Repotting: when absolutely necessary.
Compost: loam-based compost or
proprietary peat mix.
Propagation: by division in spring.
Guard against root damage.

Asplenium
Spleenwort, Bird's Nest Fern or
Mother Fern

Flowering: none.
Situation: warm, little light.
Care: water freely in summer with
rainwater, sponge leaves, feed
weekly.
Humidity: high.
Temperature: fairly high; 16–20°C
during the winter.
Repotting: in spring, if necessary.
Compost: well-sifted, airy leafmould
mixed with nutritious peat- or loam-
based compost.
Propagation: from baby plantlets, or
by division in spring.

Astrophytum
Bishop's Cap, Star Cactus or
Goat-horn Cactus

Flowering: varies according to
species.
Situation: warm in summer, cooler
and dryer in winter.
Care: water freely during growth
and provide sun-warmth; keep dry
but not cold in winter.
Humidity: low.
Temperature: minimum of 10°C.
Repotting: in spring, when necessary.
Compost: half leafmould, half sandy
soil, airy and rich in chalk; also likes
a loam- and gravel-based compost.
Propagation: from seed, possibly by
grafting.

Aucuba
Spotted Laurel

Flowering: early summer, produces
red berries after flowering.
Situation: light, no direct sunlight;
also suitable for the garden.
Care: keep fairly moist, spray
frequently, feed during the summer.
Humidity: fairly high.
Temperature: cool, but free of frost.
Repotting: in spring (not too often).
Compost: potting compost rich in
humus.
Propagation: cuttings, from seed just
after ripening.

Begonia

Flowering: varies according to
species, but usually during summer.
Situation: moderately light, screen
from direct sunlight; *B. semperflorens*
and tuber-begonias can be placed
outdoors in summer.
Care: water frequently during the
growing and flowering period with
tepid, softened water; feed weekly;
do not allow soil to dry out.
Humidity: high.
Temperature: moderate to cool.
Repotting: when necessary.
Compost: proprietary loam- or peat-
based compost.
Propagation: cuttings, leaf cuttings,
seed.

Beloperone
Shrimp Plant

Flowering: throughout the year.
Situation: light and sunny, screen from hottest sun.
Care: water freely during the growing and flowering season, feed fortnightly; can spend the summer in the garden.
Humidity: moderate.
Temperature: not below 10°C.
Repotting: in the spring.
Compost: loam-based compost or proprietary peat mix containing chalk.
Propagation: cuttings.

Bertolonia
Jewel Plant

Flowering: summer and autumn.
Situation: light and warm; shade from sun in summer.
Care: in spring and summer water with rainwater or softened tapwater, also syringe the leaves; feed every 14 days; in winter, water more sparingly and withhold feed.
Humidity: high.
Temperature: 20–24°C.
Repotting: in spring, if necessary.
Compost: bromelia compost.
Propagation: from seed.

Billbergia
Queen's Tears

Flowering: given a cool situation in winter, it will flower in late summer.
Situation: good light away from direct sunlight.
Care: water freely on top and in the funnel during summer; in winter reduce watering and move to cooler situation, keep feeding.
Humidity: moderate.
Temperature: 15–20°C.
Repotting: June, July.
Compost: leafmould with sphagnum moss; or bromelia compost.
Propagation: by division when repotting.

Blechnum
Hard Fern or Rib Fern

Flowering: none.
Situation: moderately light.
Care: water freely during growing season; do not allow soil-ball to dry out; do not spray foliage.
Humidity: very high.
Temperature: fairly warm, 15–20°C.
Repotting: in spring, if necessary.
Compost: nutritious woodland soil, rotted cow manure, some sharp sand; or an equal mixture of ordinary potting compost and peat fibre.
Propagation: from spores, by division.

Bougainvillea
Paper Flower

Flowering: spring, summer.
Situation: light and sunny.
Care: water freely during flowering, feed fortnightly, spray over crown; prune back after flowering and keep cool and dry in winter.
Humidity: high.
Temperature: warm, lots of fresh air.
Repotting: in the spring.
Compost: leafmould with loam; or proprietary loam-based compost.
Propagation: a professional grower's job.

Bouvardia
Jasmine Plant

Flowering: August–early winter.
Situation: light.
Care: water freely and feed during flowering, afterwards keep drier and cooler; provide plenty of fresh air in summer.
Humidity: moderate.
Temperature: 20°C.
Repotting: February–March.
Compost: leafmould, rotted cow manure, sharp sand; or a proprietary garden peat-based compost.
Propagation: root cuttings 3–5cms, and sideshoots of 8cms, also stem cuttings with a heel.

Brassia

Flowering: varies according to species.
Situation: March–October moderate light; October–March in the light.
Care: keep moist during the growing season, feed with a lime-free plant food every 14 days. During resting period reduce watering and place in the light.
Humidity: high.
Temperature: moderately warm greenhouse.
Repotting: in spring.
Compost: porous, fern roots and sphagnum moss; proprietary mixture for orchids.
Propagation: division.

Browallia
Amethyst, Bush Violet or Tropical Nightshade

Flowering: according to time of sowing.
Situation: light, out of full sunlight.
Care: water fairly generously, feed regularly, remove old flowers; can spend the summer in the garden.
Humidity: moderate.
Temperature: 12–16°C.
Repotting: when necessary.
Compost: leafmould with loam and rotted cow manure, or proprietary loam-based compost.
Propagation: from seed, cuttings.

Brunfelsia
Franciscan Nightshade or Kiss-me-Quick

Flowering: independent of season.
Situation: light, fairly cool, shade from direct summer sunlight.
Care: water freely during growing season, provide lots of fresh air; after flowering allow plant to rest in cool location—water sparingly and do not feed.
Humidity: moderate.
Temperature: fairly cool.
Repotting: when new growth appears.
Compost: leafmould, plenty of sharp sand, peat fibre and rotted cow manure; or proprietary peat compost.
Propagation: from seed, cuttings.

Caladium
Angel's Wings

Flowering: not at all or very rarely.
Situation: good light, out of direct sunlight.
Care: water freely, spray frequently and feed every 14 days; after growth allow the leaves to shrivel, keep tubers in the pot in a not too cold winter temperature.
Humidity: high.
Temperature: not below 18°C.
Repotting: February–March.
Compost: leafmould with peat fibre, rotted cow manure, sharp sand; or proprietary peat compost.
Propagation: from offset tubers.

Calathea
Peacock Plant

Flowering: in summer (insignificant in most species).
Situation: good light, no direct sunlight.
Care: keep compost moist, spray frequently, feed every 14 days, provide a warm environment; in winter keep drier, cooler and reduce feed.
Humidity: high.
Temperature: 12–20°C.
Repotting: spring.
Compost: loam-based potting compost.
Propagation: division, cuttings.

Calceolaria
Slipperwort, Slipper Flower, Lady's Pocketbook or Purse Flower

Flowering: spring.
Situation: light and airy, out of direct sunlight and draughts.
Care: water moderately on the soil and spray from time to time, but not too much.
Humidity: moderate.
Temperature: cool to moderately warm.
Repotting: not necessary (annual).
Compost: leafmould with sharp sand; or proprietary loam-based compost.
Propagation: from seed (difficult).

Callisia
Striped Inch Plant

Flowering: varies according to species.
Situation: not too light, no direct sunlight.
Care: keep the soil moist during growth and feed weekly; give less water and do not feed during winter.
Humidity: moderate.
Temperature: 16°C or higher.
Repotting: when necessary.
Compost: prepacked potting compost rich in humus.
Propagation: cuttings.

Callistemon
Bottle Brush Plant

Flowering: summer.
Situation: good light, warm, plenty of fresh air; outdoors in summer.
Care: water freely in summer, feed now and then, prune right back after flowering; keep cool and dry in winter.
Humidity: low.
Temperature: high, in winter 4–10°C.
Repotting: March.
Compost: friable loam-based potting compost.
Propagation: cuttings, from seed.

Camellia
Camellia

Flowering: winter–spring.
Situation: light, north-facing, outdoors in summer.
Care: keep compost moist, avoid turning pot, protect from temperature changes, alternate organic and compound fertilisers.
Humidity: moderate.
Temperature: up to 10°C in winter.
Repotting: when necessary.
Compost: loam-based compost without lime or proprietary peat mix.
Propagation: cuttings from stem or leaf-buds.

Campanula isophylla
Italian Bellflower, Bellflower or Star of Bethlehem

Flowering: summer and autumn.
Situation: good light, no direct sunlight; in the garden in summer.
Care: keep the soil moist, guard against draughts, but provide plenty of fresh air; not too warm location; remove old flowers daily.
Humidity: moderate.
Temperature: 6–8°C in the winter.
Repotting: in spring, if necessary.
Compost: leafmould with fine loam, some sharp sand; or prepacked loam-based compost.
Propagation: cuttings.

Canna
Indian Shot

Flowering: summer–autumn.
Situation: light, sunny spot, can go into sheltered position in garden after flowering.
Care: keep compost moist, feed weekly with diluted liquid fertiliser.
Humidity: moderate.
Temperature: 15°C in winter.
Repotting: early spring.
Compost: humus-rich potting compost.
Propagation: from offsets on the rootstock.

Capsicum
Pepper Plant, Christmas Pepper, Red Pepper or Chilli Plant

Flowering: summer; produces berries in autumn.
Situation: light, airy, sunny; outdoors during summer.
Care: not too much water, feed every three weeks; when buying plant, check whether insect-free; do not spray foliage during flowering.
Humidity: fairly low.
Temperature: 10–15°C in winter.
Repotting: not necessary as it is an annual.
Compost: leafmould with two parts rotted turves.
Propagation: from seed (February).

Catharanthus roseus
Madagascar Periwinkle

Flowering: spring and autumn.
Situation: light and sunny.
Care: spray regularly, keep pot and
leaves moist; feed every 14 days;
prune back in the spring.
Humidity: high.
Temperature: fairly high.
Repotting: spring, when necessary.
Compost: proprietary peat compost,
with sharp sand and rotted cow
manure.
Propagation: cuttings, from seed.

Cephalocereus
Old Man Cactus or Aztec Column

Flowering: only in the wild.
Situation: sunny and light.
Care: water only sparingly, soil
should be almost dry, quite dry from
November to February; feed with
cactus fertiliser once a fortnight;
keep in cooler place in winter.
Humidity: low.
Temperature: fairly high, not falling
under 15°C in winter.
Repotting: in spring, if necessary.
Compost: porous garden soil with
sharp sand and loam; or proprietary
cactus compost.
Propagation: from seed, cuttings.

Cereus
Torch Thistle, Column Cactus,
Hedge Cactus or Peruvian Torch

Flowering: only in the wild.
Situation: light and sunny.
Care: water freely during summer;
during resting period (winter) water
only moderately.
Humidity: low.
Temperature: fairly high, not under
10°C in winter.
Repotting: in spring, if necessary.
Compost: good garden soil, some
sharp sand and loam; or special
cactus compost.
Propagation: from seed, cuttings.

Ceropegia
Rosary Vine or String of Hearts

Flowering: in the summer.
Situation: sunny and elevated.
Care: water sparingly, feed every 14
days in the growing period.
Humidity: low, particularly in the
winter.
Temperature: 10–12°C in winter.
Repotting: in spring, if necessary.
Compost: cactus compost with some
peat fibre.
Propagation: division, cuttings, from
seed.

Chamaecereus
Peanut Cactus

Flowering: early spring.
Situation: cool, light room, little sun
in the summer.
Care: little or no water in winter;
water freely in the summer, provide
plenty of fresh air; feed with cactus
fertiliser every 2–3 weeks.
Humidity: low.
Temperature: 5–10°C in winter.
Repotting: in spring, if necessary.
Compost: cactus compost with a little
peat fibre.
Propagation: from seed, cuttings.

Chamaedorea
Dwarf Mountain or Parlour Palm

Flowering: varies according to
species.
Situation: light, not sunny.
Care: water freely with chalk-rich
water, submerge pot in water now
and then, spray frequently; feed
every 14 days; reduce water and
withhold feed in winter.
Humidity: high.
Temperature: moderately warm
room; 12–15°C in winter.
Repotting: in spring, if necessary.
Compost: leafmould with loam,
sharp sand; or loam-based compost
or prepacked peat mix.
Propagation: from seed.

Chamaerops
European Fan Palm

Flowering: summer.
Situation: sunny but no direct
sunlight; ventilate on warm days;
eventually outdoors in summer.
Care: water fairly freely in summer,
sparingly in winter; feed every 14
days in the growing period.
Humidity: moderate.
Temperature: moderately warm.
Repotting: in spring, if necessary.
Compost: loam, leafmould and sharp
sand; or prepacked loam-based
compost.
Propagation: from seed.

Chlorophytum
Spider Plant or Grass Lily

Flowering: spring–summer.
Situation: moderate light, no direct
sunlight; variegated strains need
more light.
Care: water freely during growth and
blossoming, feed and spray weekly;
reduce watering and withhold feed in
winter.
Humidity: not too low.
Temperature: 10–12°C in winter.
Repotting: when necessary.
Compost: leafmould and rotted
turves with rotted cow manure; or
loam-based compost; or proprietary
peat mix.
Propagation: from plantlets, seed or
division.

Cissus antarctica
Kangaroo Vine or Grape Ivy

Flowering: none.
Situation: light, no direct sunlight.
Care: water moderately with tepid
water and feed once a month; spray
during the winter in heated room.
Humidity: not too low.
Temperature: moderate to cool.
Repotting: in spring, if necessary.
Compost: leafmould, sharp sand,
rotted cow manure; or proprietary
loam-based compost.
Propagation: from tip cuttings and
stem sections.

Citrus
Calamondin or Seville Orange

Flowering: May; fruits in late
summer.
Situation: airy, light; cool in the
winter; can spend summer outdoors.
Care: spray daily when not in flower,
feed weekly in summer; water
sparingly in winter, but do not let
soil-ball dry out.
Humidity: not too low.
Temperature: moderately warm;
5–8°C is sufficient in winter.
Repotting: spring, if necessary.
Compost: leafmould, fine loam,
manure-peat-sand mixture; or
prepacked loam-based compost.
Propagation: only from cuttings.

Clerodendrum
Bleeding Heart Vine or Java
Glorybean

Flowering: early spring and summer.
Situation: light, no direct sunlight.
Care: water and spray daily, feed in
growing and flowering period; prune
back in the spring; provide sunnier
situation in winter and withhold feed.
Humidity: moderate.
Temperature: 10–16°C in winter.
Repotting: when necessary.
Compost: proprietary loam-based
compost or peat mix.
Propagation: cuttings, root cuttings,
sowing only with fresh seed.

Cleyera, syn. Euryea

Flowering: early spring and summer.
Situation: light, no strong sunlight.
Care: water normally in summer,
spray now and then; moderate
watering in winter; produces red
fruits.
Humidity: not too low.
Temperature: moderate to cool.
Repotting: in spring, if necessary.
Compost: leafmould, sharp sand,
rotted cow manure; or prepacked
potting compost.
Propagation: from cuttings in spring.

Clivia
Kaffir Lily

Flowering: early spring.
Situation: permanent position facing northeast or northwest.
Care: water freely during flowering season, feed weekly; keep cool in winter, water only sparingly and do not feed.
Humidity: moderate.
Temperature: 8–10°C in winter.
Repotting: after flowering, if necessary.
Compost: leafmould with garden peat, sharp sand, rotted cow manure, fine loam; or rich prepacked potting soil.
Propagation: from plantlets or seeds.

Codiaeum, syn. Croton
Jacob's Coat or South Sea Laurel

Flowering: winter, early spring.
Situation: light, sunny.
Care: spray and sponge foliage frequently, keep root-ball nicely moist, feed every two weeks; water very moderately in winter.
Humidity: high.
Temperature: not below 18°C in winter on warm base.
Repotting: in spring, if necessary.
Compost: half leafmould, half rotted cow manure or turves; or loam-based compost.
Propagation: cuttings (difficult).

Coelogyne

Flowering: according to species.
Situation: light, in spring and summer out of direct sunlight.
Care: water freely during growing period; keep in cool room in winter, pseudo-bulbs may be allowed to almost shrivel up.
Humidity: moderate.
Temperature: not below 12°C in winter.
Repotting: when the pot is filled with roots.
Compost: half sphagnum moss half fern roots (osmunda fibre), dried cow manure.
Propagation: cuttings.

Coffea
Coffee Plant

Flowering: summer, red berries.
Situation: light, airy, out of direct sunlight.
Care: water freely, spray regularly, feed weekly; allow to rest in winter but keep moist.
Humidity: high.
Temperature: high, 20–25°C during the day, not below 16°C at night.
Repotting: when necessary.
Compost: nourishing leafmould with rotted cow manure, some clay-loam; or proprietary loam-based or peat compost.
Propagation: from seed, cuttings.

Coleus
Flame Nettle, Ornamental Nettle or Painted Nettle

Flowering: according to species, summer or winter.
Situation: light, very sunny and airy.
Care: water freely in the summer, feed weekly; water less and do not feed in winter.
Temperature: fairly high.
Repotting: when necessary.
Compost: leafmould and rotted cow manure, sharp sand; or proprietary peat compost.
Propagation: cuttings, from seed.

Columnea
Goldfish Plant

Flowering: according to species.
Situation: light, no direct sunlight.
Care: keep moist during growing and flowering period, spray until buds appear and colour; give less water and do not feed in winter; keep in not too cool environment.
Humidity: high.
Temperature: 16–20°C in winter, not below 12°C at night.
Repotting: when necessary.
Compost: woodland soil, some rotted cow manure; or proprietary peat-based potting compost.
Propagation: cuttings.

Cordyline
Cabbage Palm

Flowering: sporadic, usually the more mature specimens.
Situation: good light, out of direct sunlight.
Care: spray daily, not too much direct watering, feed once a fortnight during the summer.
Humidity: high.
Temperature: always fairly high, not below 16°C in winter.
Repotting: young plants in the spring.
Compost: leafmould, rotted cow manure, peat fibre and some sharp sand; or prepacked loam-based compost or peat mix.
Propagation: from stem cuttings, root stock.

Crassula
Jade Plant

Flowering: summer (*C. falcata*) or winter (*C. arborescens*).
Situation: sunny, well ventilated.
Care: water fairly generously during flowering period, less during winter; always keep these ultra-succulent species fairly dry.
Humidity: low.
Temperature: 4–10°C in winter.
Repotting: in spring, if necessary.
Compost: nourishing and porous; leafmould, rotted cow manure, garden peat, sharp sand; or proprietary cactus soil.
Propagation: leaf and tip cuttings.

Crocus

Flowering: spring.
Situation: cool and dark during bud formation, then warmer.
Care: water sparingly, provide more and more light as the flower bud colours and grows to 5cms.
Humidity: moderate.
Temperature: moderately warm.
Repotting: pot up in September–October.
Compost: proprietary peat-based potting compost.
Propagation: nursery corms.

Crossandra
Firecracker Flower

Flowering: spring and autumn.
Situation: moderate light throughout the year.
Care: water freely with tepid water, feed every 14 days during flowering period, spray frequently; keep fairly dry and do not feed in winter.
Humidity: high.
Temperature: not falling below 12°C in winter at night, during the day 18°C.
Repotting: spring.
Compost: good proprietary peat mix or loam-based compost.
Propagation: cuttings, from seed.

Cryptanthus
Earth Star, Starfish Plant or Zebra Plant

Flowering: according to species (insignificant).
Situation: light and sunny.
Care: spray frequently, water more generously in summer than in winter: water in leaf-rosette only in summer.
Humidity: high.
Temperature: 15–18°C.
Repotting: not often; use shallow pot.
Compost: sphagnum moss, peat fibre, sharp sand, some coarse leafmould.
Propagation: division.

Ctenanthe
Never-Never Plant

Flowering: summer (insignificant).
Situation: light or moderately light, no direct sun in the summer.
Care: water freely and spray frequently in the spring and summer, feed every 14 days; water less and withhold feed in the winter.
Humidity: high.
Temperature: 18–22°C in winter.
Repotting: in the spring, if necessary.
Compost: proprietary peat-based potting compost.
Propagation: division.

Cuphea
Cigar Plant

Flowering: summer.
Situation: light and airy; can go outdoors in summer.
Care: water freely during growing and flowering period, feed occasionally; pinch out young plants to promote a bushy habit.
Humidity: moderate.
Temperature: room temperature; in winter between 10° and 16°C.
Repotting: spring.
Compost: proprietary peat-based compost.
Propagation: from seed, cuttings (usually grown annually).

Cyclamen
Sow Bread

Flowering: autumn–winter.
Situation: cool, good light, well ventilated.
Care: water freely around edges of pot or on drainage dish with tepid, soft water—remove excess water after half an hour; feed weekly; twist out dead flowers close to the corm.
Humidity: not too low.
Temperature: ideally always averaging 10–14°C.
Repotting: after the resting period, the beginning of May.
Compost: good proprietary loam-based compost.
Propagation: from seed (professional work).

Cymbidium
Orchid

Flowering: November–May.
Situation: lots of light and air, shade from the sun outdoors.
Care: keep well moist throughout the year, feed every 14 days (not in winter), keep fairly cool at night.
Humidity: fairly high.
Temperature: maximum of 20°C in winter; maximum of 30°C during the day in summer.
Repotting: in spring, after flowering.
Compost: soft and hard lumps of peat, coconut fibre, chalk; or special orchid compost.

Cyperus
Umbrella Plant

Flowering: spring–summer.
Situation: good light, no direct sunlight.
Care: must always have its roots in water—place in water-filled bowl or saucer; spray regularly, feed every 14 days during flowering period.
Humidity: high.
Temperature: moderate to cool; can go outside in its pot in summer.
Repotting: when necessary.
Compost: leafmould, mature cow manure, sharp sand, loam; or good proprietary loam-based compost.
Propagation: cuttings, division.

Cyrtomium, syn. Polystichum
Holly Fern or Shield Fern

Flowering: none.
Situation: moderate light.
Care: water freely and keep fairly warm in the summer; feed once a month and spray occasionally; keep cooler and drier in winter and do not feed.
Humidity: not too low.
Temperature: moderately warm to cool; 8–12°C is sufficient in winter.
Repotting: spring, if necessary.
Compost: leaf or pine-needle woodland soil; but can thrive in ordinary garden soil with extra humus.
Propagation: division.

Cytisus × Racemosus
Genista or Madeira Broom

Flowering: early spring–Easter.
Situation: very light and sunny.
Care: water generously during flowering period, feed fortnightly, ventilate well; can go outdoors in summer; promote flowering at 12–18°C.
Humidity: fairly high.
Temperature: 6–12°C.
Repotting: after flowering, if necessary.
Compost: leafmould, humus, sharp sand (no potting compost based on peat).
Propagation: cuttings.

Datura
Moonflower or Angel's Trumpet

Flowering: according to species.
Situation: warm and sunny.
Care: water and feed generously during growing period; outdoors in summer; the plant is very poisonous.
Humidity: fairly high.
Temperature: 10–15°C in winter.
Repotting: in spring.
Compost: leafmould, loam, mature cow manure; or loam-based potting compost.
Propagation: cuttings.

Davallia
Rabbit's Foot Fern, Squirrel's Foot Fern or Ball Fern

Flowering: none.
Situation: moderate light, warm.
Care: keep compost moist (on 'island' in water), feed very sparingly, spray.
Humidity: very high.
Temperature: not falling below 18°C in winter.
Repotting: in spring, if possible in an orchid container (creeping rootstock).
Compost: sphagnum moss, woodland soil or leafmould, some rotted cow manure; or good peat-based potting compost.
Propagation: division.

Dieffenbachia
Dumb Cane, Mother-in-Law Plant or Leopard Lily

Flowering: in the spring.
Situation: moderate light, no direct sunlight.
Care: water freely from spring onwards, spray daily; feed every 14 days; keep drier in winter, but continue spraying (water 'island').
Humidity: very high.
Temperature: 18–20°C in winter.
Repotting: in spring.
Compost: leafmould, clay or rotted turves, peat fibre, rotted cow manure; or proprietary garden peat-based compost.
Propagation: tip cuttings, 8–10cms.

Dipladenia

Flowering: spring–autumn.
Situation: light, a little sun, warm.
Care: keep moist by frequent spraying, feed every 14 days (provide air moisture—water 'island'); drier in winter .
Humidity: very high.
Temperature: fairly high, minimum of 15°C.
Repotting: in spring.
Compost: leafmould or woodland soil, clay, peat fibre, some sharp sand, rotted cow manure; or proprietary peat-based compost.
Propagation: cuttings (difficult).

Dizygotheca
False Aralia, Finger Aralia or Thread Leaf

Flowering: none.
Situation: light, not sunny.
Care: place on 'island' surrounded with water, spray daily, keep soil-ball moist, feed every 14 days (not in winter), guard against draughts.
Humidity: very high.
Temperature: not falling below 16°C in winter.
Compost: loam-based potting compost, sharp sand, fertiliser.
Repotting: early spring.
Propagation: cuttings (professional job) or from seed.

Dracaena
Dragon Tree or Corn Plant

Flowering: only mature plants in spring and autumn.
Situation: light, no direct sunlight.
Care: spray and feed regularly from March to October, keep soil-ball and surrounding air moist ('island'); drier in winter; guard against draughts.
Humidity: high.
Temperature: 16–20°C.
Repotting: in spring, if necessary.
Compost: rich, humusy potting compost (airy), rotted cow manure; or leafmould with peat.
Propagation: cuttings, from seed.

Duchesnea
Indian Strawberry

Flowering: June; fruits in July.
Situation: light and cool.
Care: keep moist during growing and flowering period, feed weekly; spray; hanging or climbing plant; produces plantlets on runners; fruits are not edible.
Humidity: moderately moist.
Temperature: room; minimum of 10°C in winter.
Repotting: in the spring, if necessary.
Compost: proprietary potting compost.
Propagation: from budding runners, from seed.

Echeveria

Flowering: according to species.
Situation: light, sunny, well-ventilated.
Care: water normally, keep dry to very dry in winter; do not spray, it is better not to feed; can go outdoors in summer (sunny).
Temperature: 6–10°C in winter.
Repotting: after flowering.
Compost: leafmould, sharp sand, chalk.
Propagation: leaf cuttings, rosette.

Echinocactus
Hedgehog Cactus or Barrel Cactus

Flowering: sporadic.
Situation: plenty of sun and warmth.
Care: water moderately during growing period in summer; drier to completely dry and cool in winter.
Humidity: low.
Temperature: not falling below 10°C in winter.
Repotting: only when strictly necessary.
Compost: cactus compost or leafmould with sharp sand and peat fibre.
Propagation: from seed.

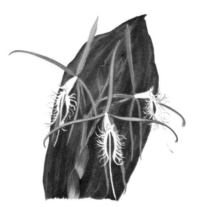

Echinocereus

Flowering: according to species.
Situation: green, profusely flowering, lightly spined species: sunny and warm; globed, thickly spined/hairy species: lots of sun, fairly dry.
Care: water the first species freely, syringe now and then; the others need watering only moderately in summer.
Humidity: low.
Temperature: 6–10°C in winter.
Repotting: when necessary.
Compost: cactus compost, available from florists.
Propagation: cuttings, from seed.

Echinopsis
Sea Urchin Cactus

Flowering: early summer, some nocturnal flowerers.
Situation: not too cold.
Care: water normally after the first bud development; can go outdoors after flowering; keep drier and cool in winter.
Humidity: low.
Temperature: 6–10°C in winter.
Repotting: in spring, if necessary.
Compost: cactus compost; rich, humusy and porous.
Propagation: cuttings, from seed.

Epidendrum
Cockle Shell Orchid

Flowering: according to species.
Situation: depending on the species: warm, moderately warm or fairly cold; light; lots of light and sun.
Care: E. medusae cool and moist, others water twice a week.
Humidity: high.
Temperature: 25–30°C (day), 14–16°C (night), lower in winter.
Repotting: after flowering.
Compost: osmunda fibre (Royal Fern roots), sphagnum moss.
Propagation: a professional job.

Epiphyllum, syn. Phyllocactus
Orchid Cactus

Flowering: spring.
Situation: light.
Care: water freely and spray after flowering; feed every 14 days; provide rest in winter (dry and cool); do not turn plant when buds are developing.
Humidity: moderately high in growing and flowering period.
Temperature: 8–12°C in winter.
Repotting: after flowering; not often.
Compost: leafmould, rotted cow manure, peat fibre, sharp sand, some clay.
Propagation: division, cuttings.

Episcia
Flame Violet or Peacock Plant

Flowering: summer and early autumn.
Situation: light, no fierce sunlight.
Care: provide atmospheric humidity by placing plant on an 'island' just above water moat; spray regularly and feed every 14 days from March to October.
Humidity: high.
Temperature: warm; not below 16°C in winter.
Repotting: in spring, if necessary.
Compost: proprietary potting compost with peat fibre.
Propagation: from cuttings (runners).

Erica
Heath, Heather

Flowering: according to species.
Situation: plenty of light, moderate sunlight.
Care: spraying regularly with rainwater is better than direct watering; feed sparingly (sensitive to salts); difficult to overwinter successfully, cool.
Humidity: not too low.
Temperature: not rising above 15°C; 5°C in winter.
Repotting: after flowering.
Compost: heath soil, sand, peat.
Propagation: cuttings (summer).

Euonymus japonicus

Flowering: May–July.
Situation: light, little sun and cool.
Care: water moderately (rather succulent leaves retain moisture), spray; feed every 14 days from spring to autumn; can spend summer outdoors.
Humidity: moderately moist.
Temperature: 10–15°C; cool in winter (5–10°C).
Repotting: early spring.
Compost: pre-packed potting compost, mature cow manure.
Propagation: cuttings of shoot tips in spring.

Euphorbia pulcherrima
Poinsettia

Flowering: winter.
Situation: permanent, plenty of light and fresh air; after April, sunny.
Care: water generously and feed every 14 days during growing period; prune back after flowering, treat wound (cigarette ash, white sand), no water.
Humidity: fairly low.
Temperature: after pruning 15–20°C.
Repotting: after flowering.
Compost: leafmould, fine loam, sharp sand, mature cow manure; or pre-packed peat- or loam-based mix.
Propagation: cuttings.

Exacum
Persian Violet or German Violet

Flowering: summer into autumn.
Situation: light, no direct sunlight.
Care: water freely during growing and flowering season, feed every 14 days, provide plenty of fresh air.
Humidity: fairly low.
Temperature: fairly cool, minimum of 4°C.
Repotting: annual.
Coupost: proprietary peat- or loam-based compost.
Propagation: possible but risky; cuttings, from seed.

Fatshedera
Tree Ivy

Flowering: autumn (rarely).
Situation: light, no sunlight.
Care: water freely, sponge foliage
weekly; feed every 14 days; plenty of
fresh air, spray occasionally; keep
drier in winter and do not feed.
Humidity: not too low.
Temperature: 18°C; in winter not
falling below 10°C.
Repotting: in spring, if necessary.
Compost: proprietary loam-based
compost, peat.
Propagation: stem cuttings, from
seed.

Fatsia
Japanese Aralia, False Castor Oil
Plant or Fig-Leaved Palm.

Flowering: autumn, mature plants.
Situation: light, no sunlight, cool.
Care: water generously in summer,
feed once a fortnight, sponge leaves
frequently; keep drier in winter.
Humidity: not too low.
Temperature: cool; 4–10°C in winter.
Repotting: in spring, if necessary.
Compost: leafmould, rotted cow
manure, sharp sand; or pre-packed
loam-based compost, or peat mix.
Propagation: cuttings in soil or water,
air-layering.

Faucaria
Tiger's Jaws

Flowering: autumn.
Situation: sunny, plenty of fresh air.
Care: water fairly generously during
growing period; keep much drier in
the resting season, plenty of light;
porous soil.
Humidity: low.
Temperature: fairly high, 8–12°C.
Repotting: after flowering, if
necessary.
Compost: coniferous woodland soil,
loam, rotted cow manure; or peat-
based potting compost.
Propagation: from seed, cuttings.

Ficus
Rubber Plant, Chinese Banyan,
Mistletoe Fig or Fiddleleaf Fig

Flowering: none.
Situation: light, morning sun.
Care: water freely (F. elastica less);
sponge regularly; feed with nutrient
solution regularly; F. pumila and
F.deltoidea require more sunlight
and a moisture atmosphere.
Humidity: according to the species.
Temperature: not falling below 12°C.
Repotting: in the spring, if necessary.
Compost: pre-packed loam-based
compost or good peat mix.
Propagation: from cuttings and
air-layering.

Fittonia
Snakeskin Plant, Mosaic Plant or
Nerve Plant

Flowering: spring (not every species).
Situation: light, no direct sunlight.
Care: evenly moist, spray daily with
softened water; feed every 14 days in
summer; keep drier in winter and
withhold feed.
Humidity: high.
Temperature: high, above 18°C.
Repotting: in the spring (shallow
container).
Compost: leafmould, peat, sharp
sand.
Propagation: in the spring from
cuttings.

Fuchsia
Lady's Eardrops

Flowering: spring–summer.
Situation: light, out of fierce sunlight,
airy; outdoors in summer.
Care: keep nice and moist in summer,
spray occasionally, feed every two
weeks; keep almost dry and cool in
winter, and do not feed.
Humidity: fairly high.
Temperature: overwinter at 10°C.
Repotting: in spring, prune.
Compost: leafmould, fertiliser, loam
or clay; or loam-based potting
compost.
Propagation: cuttings.

Gardenia
Cape Jasmine

Flowering: spring–summer and autumn.
Situation: light, sunny, warm.
Care: water generously with tepid, softened water during flowering period, spray regularly, feed with lime-free nutrient solution every two weeks, provide even warmth; keep a little drier in winter.
Humidity: very high.
Temperature: 16–22°C.
Repotting: in spring, after pruning.
Compost: leafmould, loam, sharp sand; or proprietary peat-based compost, rich and lime-free.
Propagation: in the spring, from cuttings.

Gasteria
Ox-Tongue or Cape Hart's Tongue

Flowering: summer.
Situation: light, moderately sunny.
Care: water fairly freely and feed every 14 days in summer; keep cool and almost dry in winter.
Humidity: low.
Temperature: moderately warm room, 10–12°C.
Repotting: in spring, if necessary.
Propagation: cuttings, from seed.

Gloriosa
Gloriosa Lily or Glory Lily

Flowering: late summer.
Situation: plenty of light, full sunlight.
Care: keep compost with germinating tuber well moistened; spray frequently during flowering season; when flowers have died allow tubers to ripen off for two months, lift and keep dry.
Humidity: high, when in flower.
Temperature: 30°C during growing period, then 20°C.
Repotting: in the early spring.
Propagation: young bulbs.

Grevillea
Silk Oak

Flowering: none; mature plants sometimes flower.
Situation: moderate light, no direct sunlight.
Care: regular, but not too much water and fertiliser (quicker growth); spray regularly; keep cool in winter.
Humidity: not too low.
Temperature: cool room; 7–10°C in winter.
Repotting: young plant every spring.
Compost: leafmould, rotted cow manure, sharp sand; or good pre-packed potting compost.
Propagation: from seed in spring.

Guzmania
Orange Star

Flowering: winter.
Situation: warm, light, no sunlight.
Care: place on an 'island' in water; water also in the funnel in summer; spray frequently, feed every 14 days.
Humidity: very high.
Temperature: 20–22°C, not falling below 18°C.
Repotting: when parent plant dies off.
Compost: orchid soil.
Propagation: from young offshoots at base of plant.

Gymnocalycium
Spider Cactus

Flowering: according to species.
Situation: light, no fierce sunlight.
Care: water freely during growing period; keep cool in winter (8°C), also dry.
Humidity: low.
Temperature: varies according to the species—8–12°C.
Repotting: not necessary.
Compost: alkali-free, porous potting compost.
Propagation: from seed, offset cuttings; some strains need to be grafted, otherwise they grow very little or not at all.

Gynura
Purple Passion Vine or Velvet Plant

Flowering: autumn (rarely).
Situation: light, sunny and airy.
Care: water generously and feed only
occasionally in summer; keep
somewhat drier in winter.
Humidity: moderate.
Temperature: warm, above 20°C in
summer, 15–18°C during the winter.
Repotting: March (large pot).
Compost: proprietary peat- or loam-
based compost; or rotted cow
manure, loam.
Propagation: cuttings (10cms).

Haemanthus
Blood Lily, White Paint Brush or
Fireball

Flowering: summer.
Situation: light, sunny and airy.
Care: plant bulbs in March; do not
water over bulb; water and spray
freely during growing period, drier
thereafter; feed only during summer.
Humidity: low.
Temperature: 10–15°C in winter.
Repotting: better not to; if necessary
in February–March; set bulb only
half way into the compost.
Compost: good loam-based compost;
or leafmould, rotted cow manure,
loam.
Propagation: by offsets from the
bulbs.

Haworthia

Flowering: spring–summer.
Situation: light, little sunlight.
Care: water moderately over the soil,
feed every 14 days; keep cool and
fairly dry in winter.
Humidity: low.
Temperature: moderately warm to
cool; 8–12°C in winter.
Repotting: in spring (shallow
container).
Compost: humusy leafmould, loam,
sharp sand; or prepacked cactus soil.
Propagation: offset cuttings; or from
seed.

Hebe
Veronica

Flowering: autumn.
Situation: light, not too warm.
Care: water moderately, prune back
after flowering; keep cool in winter;
can go into the garden from early
summer to October.
Humidity: moderate.
Temperature: cool, 8–12°C in winter.
Repotting: spring.
Compost: leafmould, loam, rotted
cow manure; or pre-packed loam-
based compost.
Propagation: cuttings, preferably
with a heel.

Hedera
Ivy

Flowering: seldom in a living room.
Situation: light to moderately light.
Care: water moderately and spray
occasionally; feed once every 2–3
weeks; keep drier and do not feed in
winter.
Humidity: not too low.
Temperature: around 12°C in winter.
Repotting: in spring (keep to
smallish pot).
Compost: garden soil, rotted cow
manure, leafmould; or potting
compost.
Propagation: cuttings (10–15cms).

Hemigraphis
Red Ivy

Flowering: summer (insignificant).
Situation: light, no direct sunlight.
Care: water freely during growing
and flowering period, spray twice a
week, feed every two weeks; keep
drier but spray occasionally with
tepid water in winter.
Humidity: high (provide a water
'island').
Temperature: above 16°C.
Repotting: in the spring (roomy pot).
Compost: potting compost, peat.
Propagation: from stems with leaf-
buds attached, cuttings.

Hibiscus
Rose of China or Chinese Rose

Flowering: summer–autumn.
Situation: light, warm, sunny (no direct sunlight), permanent location.
Care: plenty of fresh air, water fairly generously, spray, feed weekly; drier and no fertiliser in the winter.
Humidity: high.
Temperature: around 12°C in winter.
Repotting: once every 2–3 years.
Compost: leafmould, sharp sand, well-rotted cow manure; or loam-based compost.
Propagation: cuttings.

Hippeastrum
Amaryllis

Flowering: winter–spring.
Situation: depending on growing stage: darker, lighter, sunny.
Care: increase watering gradually as flower bud appears; feed weekly and provide sunny position; continue watering and feeding after flowering, to promote growth of bulb; allow plant to rest from October to December, keep dry and cool.
Humidity: low.
Temperature: when flowering 20°C, when resting 16°C.
Repotting: November–February.
Compost: loam-based compost, peat.
Propagation: offset bulbs, from seed.

Howeia, syn. Kentia
Kentia Palm

Flowering: only mature plants.
Situation: light—moderately light, no sunlight, moist.
Care: water freely between February and October, spray, immerse in water occasionally, feed twice a month; in winter provide moderate, even temperature and do not feed.
Humidity: high.
Temperature: min. of 12°C in winter.
Repotting: only when strictly necessary (deep palm pot).
Compost: leafmould, rotted manure, some sharp sand; or pre-packed humusy potting compost.
Propagation: from seed (professional job).

Hoya
Wax Plant, Porcelain Flower or Shower of Stars

Flowering: occasionally twice a year.
Situation: plenty of light, no direct sunlight.
Care: hanging or climbing plant; feed every 14 days during growing and flowering period, water generously, spray; keep fairly dry in winter; turn plant as little as possible.
Humidity: fairly high.
Temperature: 12–15°C in winter.
Repotting: only if absolutely necessary, in spring.
Compost: leafmould, humus, loam; or proprietary loam-based compost.
Propagation: cuttings.

Hyacinthus
Hyacinth

Flowering: spring, or Christmas (forced).
Situation: dark, cool until shoot is around 7cms long, then lighter.
Care: water daily; keep pot in the dark until flower bud has developed, then lighter, warmer (under plastic); with soilless cultivation, place bulb 2mm above water, cool.
Humidity: high.
Temperature: when flowering 18–20°C.
Repotting: September–October.
Compost: pre-packed compost (loam- or peat-based), $\frac{1}{4}$ sand.
Propagation: not in the home.

Hydrangea

Flowering: spring and late summer.
Situation: cool, no sunlight, moderate light; outdoors in summer.
Care: move to warmer location at the end of February; water and feed twice a week during flowering period; prune back after flowering.
Humidity: fairly low.
Temperature: 5–10°C from autumn onwards.
Repotting: after flowering.
Compost: rotted turves, humusy peat; also thrives in pre-packed potting compost with some extra peat fibre.
Propagation: cuttings (10cms).

Hymenocallis
Spider Lily or Lily Basket

Flowering: according to the species, in summer or autumn.
Situation: light, no fierce sunlight.
Care: increase watering as growth progresses; feed twice a month, not in winter, also reduce watering; sponge foliage.
Humidity: not too low.
Temperature: overwinters at 15°C.
Repotting: once in every 2–3 years.
Compost: fine clay-loam, rotted cow manure, sharp sand; or proprietary loam-based compost.
Propagation: offset bulbs.

Hypocyrta
Clog Plant

Flowering: summer.
Situation: light, eventually some sunlight.
Care: water fairly freely in summer, moderately with tepid water in winter; feed twice a month; do not prune, only remove old stems that have grown too wild, in June.
Humidity: fairly high.
Temperature: cool room, 10–15°C in winter.
Repotting: in the spring, if necessary.
Compost: leafmould, peat fibre.
Propagation: division, from seed, cuttings.

Hypoestes
Freckleface or Polka Dot Plant

Flowering: summer.
Situation: light, warm, some sun.
Care: water normally throughout the year, spray regularly; guard against draughts; keep drier during resting period.
Humidity: very high.
Temperature: 15–20°C.
Repotting: in spring (shallow pot).
Compost: humusy loam- or peat-based compost, or leafmould with rotted cow manure.
Propagation: cuttings.

Impatiens
Busy Lizzie, Water Fuchsia, Dusky Lizzie or Patient Lucy

Flowering: in every season.
Situation: light, no direct sunlight.
Care: plenty of fresh air, keep well moist (lime-free water), feed frequently during growing period, spray leaves occasionally but not over flowers.
Humidity: moderate.
Temperature: living room.
Repotting: every spring, after flowering.
Compost: pre-packed potting compost, some rotted cow manure.
Propagation: cuttings, from seed; old plants often grow unsightly.

Ipomoea
Morning Glory

Flowering: throughout the summer.
Situation: plenty of light and sunshine.
Care: lots of fresh air, spray frequently, water generously, feed weekly; can eventually go outdoors in summer; fast grower that needs to be trained; one day flowerer.
Humidity: not too low.
Temperature: moderately warm room.
Repotting: not necessary (annual).
Compost: chalky compost, organic fertiliser.
Propagation: from seeds, March–April.

Iresine
Bloodleaf

Flowering: summer (insignificant).
Situation: warm, in the sunshine, moist; can go outdoors in summer.
Care: keep soil well moistened, spray frequently (rainwater), feed fortnightly with houseplant fertiliser; occasional topping encourages bushier growth.
Humidity: moderate.
Temperature: warm room, minimum of 10–15°C in winter.
Repotting: in spring, if necessary.
Compost: loam-based compost; or proprietary peat mix.
Propagation: cuttings (6–10cms).

Ixora
Flame of the Woods or Indian Jasmine

Flowering: July–September.
Situation: warm, moderately sunny or sunless during growing and flowering period.
Care: spray every two weeks until flowering begins, keep soil moist; feed every two weeks (not winter); place in winter sun and keep drier.
Humidity: high.
Temperature: 15–20°C.
Repotting: biannually, in spring.
Compost: proprietary loam- or peat-based compost.
Propagation: cuttings (10–15cms).

Jacaranda

Flowering: not in European climate.
Situation: warm, light to moderately light.
Care: water moderately, less in winter, feed every two weeks with lime-free nutrient solution during growing period.
Humidity: high.
Temperature: 20°C; minimum of 16°C in winter.
Repotting: in the spring.
Compost: proprietary loam-based compost or humusy peat mix.
Propagation: from seed.

Jacobinia

Flowering: summer.
Situation: light, sunny (no fierce sunlight), even warmth.
Care: water freely during summer with lime-free water, spray, feed fortnightly; withhold feed and keep drier in winter.
Humidity: high (water 'island').
Temperature: warm room; minimum of 15–18°C in the winter.
Repotting: in spring, if necessary.
Compost: pre-packed potting compost with clay-loam.
Propagation: cuttings (approx. 8cms).

Jasminum
Jasmine

Flowering: summer–autumn.
Situation: light, sunny, not warm.
Care: feed and spray regularly, water freely during flowering period; can go outdoors in summer; keep drier in winter; prune back in spring.
Humidity: fairly high.
Temperature: 12–20°C.
Repotting: spring or autumn.
Compost: potting compost, peat, rotted cow manure.
Propagation: cuttings (taken when pruning).

Kalanchoe
Flaming Katy

Flowering: according to the species.
Situation: cool, light, little sun in the summer, sunny location in winter.
Care: water sparingly, feed monthly, plenty of fresh air; keep fairly dry in winter; prune back after flowering.
Humidity: not too low.
Temperature: cool room.
Repotting: when necessary.
Compost: loam-based compost with peat fibre and sharp sand.
Propagation: tip, leaf and side-shoot cuttings, from seed, and offsets.

Kohleria, syn. Tydaea

Flowering: summer.
Situation: light, no direct sunlight.
Care: water fairly freely and feed every one or two weeks, set plant on an 'island' in water; keep moderately moist in winter and withhold feed.
Humidity: fairly high.
Temperature: 8–15°C in winter.
Repotting: in the spring, if necessary.
Compost: humusy leafmould or loam-based compost, rotted cow manure.
Propagation: by dividing the rootstock (rhizome) or taking stem cuttings, from seed.

Lachenalia
Cape Cowslip

Flowering: according to the species; usually in spring.
Situation: light, cool.
Care: water sparingly to begin with, gradually increase as growth progresses; feed every three weeks, ventilate well; allow to rest after flowering.
Humidity: moderate.
Temperature: pot up at 12°C.
Repotting: after flowering, September–October.
Compost: leafmould, loam, sharp sand and rotted cow manure; or proprietary loam-based compost.
Propagation: offset bulbs (bulbils).

Laurus
Bay Tree

Flowering: in spring (insignificant).
Situation: light, no sunlight, fresh air; can go outdoors in summer.
Care: provide winter rest by keeping cool and (almost) dry; prune back in August–September; spray daily during growing period, feed fortnightly and water freely.
Humidity: high.
Temperature: overwinter at 3–8°C.
Repotting: early spring.
Compost: leafy garden compost, loam; or pre-packed loam-based compost.
Propagation: cuttings.

Lilium
Lily

Flowering: at any season of the year.
Situation: warmer as growth progresses; light, plenty of fresh air.
Care: steadily increase watering as growth increases, feed every 14 days; keep moist but not too wet.
Humidity: moderate.
Temperature: from 10° to approx. 17°C.
Repotting: preferably in autumn.
Compost: leafmould, peat, sharp sand; or proprietary loam-based compost or peat mix.
Propagation: non-prepared bulbs are perennial.

Lycaste

Flowering: winter–spring.
Situation: light, cool in the winter, warm in summer.
Care: keep well moist during growing period, feed monthly; spray moderately, keep almost dry in winter so that pseudo bulbs will not shrivel.
Humidity: high.
Temperature: 18–22°C in summer; not below 10–12°C in winter.
Repotting: after flowering, in spring.
Compost: equal parts sphagnum moss, osmunda fibre, leafmould and loam.
Propagation: from seed (professional job).

Mammillaria
Pincushion Cactus

Flowering: summer, after which it sometimes fruits.
Situation: most species enjoy the sunshine.
Care: water fairly freely over the soil in summer; keep almost dry during the winter; cactus fertiliser in the summer.
Humidity: low.
Temperature: 6–10°C in winter.
Repotting: when necessary.
Compost: garden compost, sharp sand, fine clay; or pre-packed cactus soil.
Propagation: from seed, sometimes from cuttings.

Manettia
Firecracker Plant

Flowering: spring–summer–autumn.
Situation: light, warm, some sunshine.
Care: hanging or climbing plant; water generously, feed weekly; keep much drier in winter, cooler; ventilate well.
Humidity: high (water 'island').
Temperature: not falling below 12–15°C in winter.
Repotting: young plants every spring.
Compost: good loam-based compost or humusy peat mix.
Propagation: from cuttings in spring.

Maranta
Arrowroot, Prayer Plant or
Rabbit Track Plant

Flowering: only very mature plants
in spring and summer (insignificant).
Situation: good light but out of the
sun.
Care: spray frequently, also in the
winter (instead of watering on the
soil), feed every 14 days during
growing period.
Humidity: high.
Temperature: 22°C; minimum of
16°C.
Repotting: in spring, if necessary.
Compost: leafmould, peat, rotted
cow manure; or loam-based compost
or garden peat mix.
Propagation: by division.

Medinilla

Flowering: spring–summer.
Situation: light, warm, provide
atmospheric humidity ('island'), no
fierce sunlight.
Care: keep compost moist during
growing and flowering period, feed
twice a month; keep drier and cooler
in winter and do not feed.
Humidity: very high.
Temperature: 20–25°C; 16°C in
winter.
Repotting: in spring, if necessary.
Compost: potting compost, peat
fibre, sphagnum moss.
Propagation: cuttings.

Mesembryanthemum

Flowering: according to the species,
only in the sun.
Situation: warm and sunny.
Care: water (not too freely) as soon
as young leaves appear, gradually
reduce watering as the leaves shrivel;
ventilate well.
Humidity: low.
Temperature: minimum of 5–10°C in
winter.
Repotting: seldom.
Compost: porous, non-acid, not too
nourishing.
Propagation: cuttings, from seed.

Microcoelum
Coconut Palm

Flowering: none.
Situation: warm, good light but out
of the sun.
Care: water liberally when growing,
spray regularly, immerse
occasionally, feed every 14 days;
keep drier and do not feed in winter.
Humidity: high.
Temperature: 15–18°C in the winter.
Repotting: only when strictly
necessary.
Compost: loam, leafmould, sharp
sand; or pre-packed potting compost.
Propagation: spores (professional
grower's work).

Microlepia

Flowering: none.
Situation: moderate light, no
sunlight, warm and moist.
Care: spray regularly, feed every 14
days, water freely in summer; keep
drier in winter and withhold feed.
Humidity: very high.
Temperature: minimum of 15°C.
Repotting: in the spring, if necessary.
Compost: leafmould, rotted cow
manure, sharp sand; or proprietary
peat-based compost.
Propagation: spores (professional
grower's work).

Miltonia
Pansy Orchid

Flowering: according to the species.
Situation: no direct sunlight, fairly
good light; plenty of sunlight in
winter.
Care: water twice a week throughout
the year, keep soil moist; feed with
orchid fertiliser twice a month in
summer; spray moderately.
Humidity: high.
Temperature: 18–22°C.
Repotting: September.
Compost: sphagnum moss, peat,
osmunda fibre.
Propagation: division, from seed.

Mimosa
Sensitive Plant or Humble Plant

Flowering: spring–autumn.
Situation: light and sunny.
Care: plenty of fresh air; water
liberally during growing and
flowering period; feed every 14 days;
keep fairly dry and do not feed in
winter; plant is difficult to keep into
maturity.
Humidity: fairly high.
Temperature: min. of 12°C in winter.
Repotting: spring.
Compost: leafmould, sharp sand,
rotted cow manure; or proprietary
loam-based compost.
Propagation: from seed in the spring.

Monstera
Swiss Cheese Plant, Mexican Bread
Fruit or Splitleaf Philodendron

Flowering: only mature plants.
Situation: moderate light, warm.
Care: water freely during growing
period; feed every 14 days from
March to November; sponge leaves
regularly.
Humidity: high.
Temperature: 12–20°C in winter.
Repotting: in spring, if necessary.
Compost: leafmould, rotted cow
manure, sharp sand; or loam-based
compost or proprietary peat mix.
Propagation: cuttings taken in
summer.

Musa acuminata
Dwarf Banana

Flowering: summer; Nov–Dec,
fruits.
Situation: warm, very good light.
Care: water liberally in spring and
and autumn; feed every 2 to 3 weeks;
spray foliage throughout the year;
keep drier and do not feed in winter.
Humidity: high.
Temperature: above 20°C; 8–12°C
in winter.
Repotting: plant dies off; offshoot
suckers.
Compost: nourishing; leafmould,
loam, rotted cow manure, sharp
sand; or good loam-based compost.
Propagation: rootstock division.

Myrtus
Myrtle

Flowering: summer, berries appear
in autumn.
Situation: light, cool; can go
outdoors in summer.
Care: water freely with lime-free
water during growing period; feed
occasionally; spray but water
moderately in autumn, withhold feed.
Humidity: moderate.
Temperature: 5–8°C in winter.
Repotting: in spring, if necessary.
Compost: lime-free leafmould, fine
loam and rotted cow manure; or
pre-packed loam-based compost.
Propagation: cuttings.

Neoregelia
Air Pine or Blushing Bromeliad

Flowering: at centre of plant
(insignificant).
Situation: good light but out of direct
sunlight.
Care: spray regularly, also in the
centre funnel; feed every fortnight;
keep moist but do not feed in winter.
Humidity: high, drier in winter.
Temperature: 23°C; winter min. 15°C.
Repotting: in spring (shallow
container).
Compost: leafmould, rotted cow
manure, sphagnum moss; or
bromelia soil.
Propagation: division of rooted
offsets in summer.

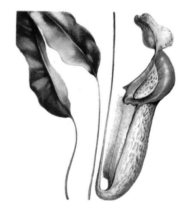

Nepenthes
Dutchman's Pipe or Pitcher Plant

Flowering: none; 'pitcher' has hairy
honey glands near the mouth
(insectivorous).
Situation: plenty of light but no
direct sunlight; warm, humid.
Care: keep moist from spring to
autumn, drier in winter and cooler;
difficult climber.
Humidity: very high.
Temperature: around 25°C.
Repotting: February–March.
Compost: special orchid soil; or
sphagnum moss with osmunda fibre.
Propagation: cuttings from well-
ripened shoots.

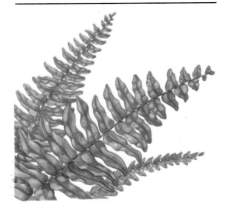

Nephrolepis
Sword Fern or Boston Fern

Flowering: none.
Situation: moderate light, not too warm.
Care: water liberally, spray frequently, feed twice a month; keep drier and feed less in winter, spray every other week.
Humidity: high in summer.
Temperature: 16–18°C, minimum of 14°C in the winter.
Repotting: not often; spring.
Compost: leafmould, humusy peat, rotted cow manure, sharp sand.
Propagation: divide young shoots on the runners.

Nerine
Guernsey Lily

Flowering: late summer or autumn.
Situation: good light but no fierce sunlight.
Care: keep soil-ball moist when plant is growing; lift bulb after flowering and keep at 5°C, max. 13°C; keep *N. sarniensis*-bulb at 17–20°C.
Humidity: fairly high.
Temperature: 12–16°C during flowering period.
Repotting: January–June.
Compost: porous mixture; leafmould with sharp sand; or proprietary loam-based compost.
Propagation: bulb offsets, from seed.

Nerium
Oleander

Flowering: summer, from June onwards.
Situation: good light, sunlight, plenty of fresh air.
Care: keep moist during growing period; water freely, feed weekly, spray; check that pot has good drainage; cooler and drier from autumn and no feed; poisonous!
Humidity: low.
Temperature: 18–25°C; winter minimum of 5°C.
Repotting: young plants in the spring.
Compost: clay or loam, rotted cow manure, peat, sharp sand.
Propagation: cuttings in water.

Nertera
Bead Plant or Coral Moss

Flowering: spring, followed by berries.
Situation: light, no fierce sunlight.
Care: sunny in the winter; feed every 14 days when flowering; water moderately on the drainage dish; pollinate with fine brush; ventilate well.
Humidity: moderate.
Temperature: 16°C; approximately 10–12°C in winter.
Repotting: in the spring (use shallow pot).
Compost: leafmould, rotted cow manure, sharp sand.
Propagation: by division.

Nidularium
Bird's Nest Bromeliad

Flowering: summer, insignificant flowers, bud-shaped.
Situation: warm, moist air, moderate light.
Care: water freely in the summer, also in the leaf funnel, feed fortnightly; keep drier and do not feed in winter.
Humidity: high ('island').
Temperature: minimum of 15°C.
Repotting: eventually in the spring.
Compost: leafmould, rotted cow manure, sphagnum moss.
Propagation: by offsets removed in late spring or summer.

Notocactus
Goldfinger Cactus

Flowering: summer.
Situation: good light, warm, sunny.
Care: moderately moist in the summer, drier and somewhat cooler in winter; spray occasionally in summer with tepid water, in the mornings only when it is sunny weather; feed occasionally with cactus fertiliser.
Humidity: low.
Temperature: not below 12°C in winter.
Repotting: when necessary.
Compost: sandy, well-draining soil, some leafmould.
Propagation: from seed; cuttings.

Odontoglossum
Lace Orchid or Tiger Orchid

Flowering: according to the species.
Situation: cool, good light but no
direct sunlight, plenty of fresh air and
moist atmosphere.
Care: (Central American species)
water freely during growing period,
May–Oct, spray foliage, feed every
14 days; keep dry and cool Nov–Apr.
Humidity: high (water 'island').
Temperature: 15–17°C; not above
7°C in winter.
Repotting: after flowering, not often;
young shoot at least 4 cms long.
Compost: fern roots, sphagnum moss;
or pre-packed orchid soil.
Propagation: by division.

Olea
Olive

Flowering: spring, summer.
Situation: strong sunlight, dry
atmosphere.
Care: undemanding plant; water very
sparingly, ensure good drainage; can
go outdoors in summer, lime-rich
soil.
Humidity: very low.
Temperature: can be fairly high.
Repotting: only occasionally.
Compost: potting compost with
added lime.
Propagation: cuttings (take a long
time).

Oncidium
Dancing Doll Orchid or
Butterfly Orchid

Flowering: according to the species.
Situation: good light but no full
sunlight.
Care: water freely during growing
period, March–Oct; feed with
orchid fertiliser every fortnight; keep
almost dry for one month during
winter; cold greenhouse varieties—
cooler, moister atmosphere.
Humidity: high.
Temperature: 18–22°C; not below
12°C in winter.
Repotting: after flowering.
Compost: fern roots, sphagnum moss.
Propagation: by division.

Ophiopogon
Snake's Beard, Lily Turf or
Mondo Grass

Flowering: summer, followed by
berries.
Situation: light, eventually semi-
shade; variegated varieties more
light, some sun.
Care: undemanding plant; water
freely when growing and flowering
and feed every fortnight; keep drier
and cooler in winter without feed.
Humidity: moderate.
Temperature: 20–25°C, can be cooler;
10°C in the winter.
Repotting: spring, if necessary.
Compost: proprietary peat mix.
Propagation: in spring, by division.

Oplismenus
Basket Grass

Flowering: (insignificant) in the
summer.
Situation: warm, good light in the
summer, moderate light in winter.
Care: water regularly in the summer
and feed fortnightly; spray in the
winter and do not feed.
Humidity: high.
Temperature: 10–20°C in winter.
Repotting: in spring, if necessary.
Compost: leafmould, peat fibre; or
proprietary peat compost.
Propagation: cuttings, by division.

Opuntia
Prickly Pear or Bunny Ears

Flowering: spring–summer.
Situation: warm and sunny; light and
cool in winter.
Care: water normally during growing
period and feed every 14 days with
cactus fertiliser, then gradually
reduce watering and allow to rest
almost dry in the winter.
Humidity: low.
Temperature: approx. 7°C in winter,
about 20°C at other times.
Repotting: spring, if necessary.
Compost: porous and rich; special
proprietary cactus soil, for instance.
Propagation: cuttings, eventually
from seed.

Oxalis
Lucky Clover, Wood Sorrel or
Bermuda Buttercup.

Flowering: summer–autumn.
Situation: good light, some sunshine,
fairly cool; can go outdoors in
summer.
Care: water moderately, increase as
renewed growth appears; feed once
every 2–3 weeks; lift tubers in
autumn and store dry.
Humidity: moderate.
Temperature: 18°C, in winter 4–8°C.
Repotting: pot up in Jan–Feb.
Compost: lime-free, sandy compost.
Propagation: bulb offsets.

Pachyphytum
Moonstones or Sticky Moonstones

Flowering: summer.
Situation: sunny, plenty of fresh air
in the summer.
Care: water moderately in summer,
definitely not on the leaves; keep
drier and cooler in winter.
Humidity: low.
Temperature: 10°C in winter.
Repotting: in spring, if necessary.
Compost: nourishing potting
compost mixed with sharp sand.
Propagation: tip or leaf cuttings,
from seed.

Pachystachys
Gold Hops or Lollipop Plant

Flowering: spring–summer.
Situation: light, no direct sunlight
but plenty of fresh air.
Care: keep fairly moist during
growing and flowering period. and
feed fortnightly; no feed and drier in
winter.
Humidity: fairly high.
Temperature: around 15°C in winter.
Repotting: spring, if necessary.
Compost: peat-based potting
compost, rotted cow manure.
Propagation: cuttings at 20–25°C.

Pandanus
Screw Pine

Flowering: none.
Situation: warm, humid, light, no
strong sunlight.
Care: water freely but only with
tepid water when growing; spray
frequently and feed once a fortnight;
keep drier and withhold feed in
winter.
Humidity: very high.
Temperature: 23°C; winter min. 16°C.
Repotting: young plants in the spring.
Compost: proprietary potting
compost; or leafmould or sphagnum
moss with fine clay or loam.
Propagation: runners, from seed.

Paphiopedilum
Slipper Orchid or Lady's Slipper

Flowering: according to the species.
Situation: no sunlight, full light in
winter, shade in summer.
Care: keep moist when flowering,
feed fortnightly; spray until flowers
appear.
Humidity: high (provide extra
humidity—'island').
Temperature: 18°C; winter min.
12°C; marbled leaf strains, warmer.
Repotting: in spring, after flowering.
Compost: osmunda fibre, sphagnum
moss, coarse (beech) leafmould
(airy).
Propagation: by division when
repotting.

Passiflora
Passion Flower

Flowering: summer–autumn.
Situation: plenty of sunlight, fresh
air; can go outdoors in summer.
Care: water generously, feed every
14 days; keep drier and withhold feed
in the winter.
Humidity: moderate.
Temperature: 6–10°C in winter.
Repotting: spring.
Compost: potting compost, peat,
mature cow manure; or leafmould,
sand.
Propagation: cuttings in water or
rooting compost.

Pavonia

Flowering: November–March.
Situation: plenty of light but no
strong sunlight.
Care: water liberally, spray
occasionally and feed every 14 days;
water moderately in winter and
withhold feed.
Humidity: fairly high.
Temperature: 16–20°C.
Repotting: in spring.
Compost: proprietary peat-based
compost with some mature cow
manure.
Propagation: cuttings (difficult),
topping should only take place
above 25°C, from seed.

Pedilanthus
Ribbon Cactus or Redbird Cactus

Flowering: only mature plants,
flowering insignificant.
Situation: good light, out of direct
sunlight.
Care: water only when compost feels
dry; keep drier in winter; loses leaves
in autumn; plant has poisonous sap!
Humidity: low.
Temperature: 12–20°C.
Repotting: in spring, if necessary.
Compost: leafmould, clay, sharp
sand; or proprietary loam-based
compost or peat mix.
Propagation: cuttings taken in the
summer.

Pelargonium
Geranium

Flowering: summer (prolonged).
Situation: good light, sunny, lots of
fresh air; can go outdoors in summer.
Care: water moderately, do not
spray, feed weekly when growing;
keep drier in winter.
Humidity: low.
Temperature: fairly cool; 5–10°C in
winter.
Repotting: spring.
Compost: sandy leafmould, mature
cow manure, some fine loam; or
proprietary loam-based compost.
Propagation: stem-tip cuttings in late
summer, from seed.

Pellaea
Button Fern

Flowering: none—ferns do not
Situation: no sunlight, (moderate)
light, airy.
Care: keep soil nice and moist, spray
regularly and feed every 14 days;
water more sparingly in winter.
Humidity: not too low, can possibly
be placed on a water 'island' in winter.
Temperature: winter min. of 10–12°C.
Repotting: spring (shallow
container).
Compost: leafmould, peat, rotted
cow manure; or fern compost.
Propagation: by division.

Pellionia

Flowering: none.
Situation: shady, warm.
Care: water generously with
rainwater and feed weekly; keep
somewhat drier in winter.
Humidity: very high (set on an
'island' in water).
Temperature: winter minimum
around 12°C.
Repotting: spring (wide container).
Compost: airy leafmould compost; or
proprietary peat mix.
Propagation: from cuttings in spring.

Peperomia
Pepper Elder or Watermelon
Peperomia

Flowering: according to the species.
Situation: good light, no direct
sunlight, warm.
Care: water moderately, feed every
14 days; spray occasionally in winter
with tepid water and withhold feed.
Humidity: high ('island').
Temperature: 17–20°C; not below
12°C in winter.
Repotting: only when strictly
necessary.
Compost: leafmould, sharp sand,
rotted cow manure; or pre-packed
loam-based or peat compost.
Propagation: stem-tip or leaf cuttings.

Pereskia
Barbados Gooseberry or Lemon Vine

Flowering: cultivated species seldom flower.
Situation: humid and warm, good light.
Care: keep moist and humid when growing, feed every 2–3 weeks; drier in winter; no moisture or feed from leaf-fall to regrowth.
Humidity: high.
Temperature: 10–12°C in winter.
Repotting: spring, if necessary (preferably in plastic pot).
Compost: leafmould or garden peat compost, clay, rotted cow manure.
Propagation: cuttings.

Peristrophe

Flowering: according to the species.
Situation: warm, light, no sunlight.
Care: water liberally, spray foliage, feed every 14 days; spray in winter rather than watering on the soil and do not feed.
Humidity: high.
Temperature: not falling below 15°C in winter; averaging 20–23°C during the day and in summer.
Repotting: spring.
Compost: pre-packed potting compost, peat.
Propagation: cuttings.

Philodendron
Sweetheart Plant, Heart-leaf Philodendron or Sweetheart Vine

Flowering: flowers insignificant.
Situation: warm in summer, cool in winter.
Care: water freely between spring and August with luke-warm water, feed monthly; keep drier in winter and do not feed.
Humidity: high.
Temperature: 16–24°C during the day; variegated and hairy species not below 18°C.
Repotting: infrequently; in the spring.
Compost: coarse leafmould, loam turf soil, sharp sand and rotted cow manure.
Propagation: cuttings.

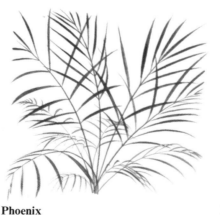

Phlebodium

Flowering: none.
Situation: moderately light and warm.
Care: keep compost moist with soft water, spray regularly, feed every 14 days; water only moderately in winter and withhold feed.
Humidity: high (set on water 'island').
Temperature: not below 16–18°C in winter.
Repotting: spring, if necessary.
Compost: leafy peat, rotted cow manure, sharp sand; or pre-packed fern compost.
Propagation: by division, rootstock sections, from seed (professional job).

Phoenix
Canary Date Palm or Pygmy Date Palm

Flowering: cultivated species do not usually flower.
Situation: light and warm from spring to autumn; cool in winter.
Care: water freely during growing period and feed fortnightly; spray frequently; keep drier in winter and withhold feed, but continue spraying.
Humidity: moderate.
Temperature: min 5–10°C in winter.
Repotting: not often; in spring.
Compost: loamy soil, leafmould, sharp sand, no peat; or pre-packed loam-based compost.
Propagation: from seed, by division.

Pilea
Aluminium Plant or Friendship Plant

Flowering: insignificant blooms.
Situation: fairly warm and sunny; can spend the summer in the garden under the sun.
Care: water fairly generously in summer and feed every 14 days; keep drier in winter and do not feed.
Humidity: high.
Temperature: room temperature; not below 10°C in winter.
Repotting: spring, if necessary.
Compost: proprietary loam-based compost or peat mix.
Propagation: cuttings (in water).

Piper
Pepper

Flowering: rarely.
Situation: moderate light;
P. ornatum more light, no fierce
sunlight.
Care: keep soil moist but not wet,
spray, feed fortnightly; keep drier in
winter and feed every other month.
Humidity: high (set on water 'island').
Temperature: not below 12°C in
winter.
Repotting: in spring, if necessary.
Compost: leafmould, rotted cow
manure, sharp sand; or pre-packed
potting compost.
Propagation: cuttings, from seed.

Pisonia, syn. Heimerliodendron

Flowering: seldom flowers in home
cultivation.
Situation: good light, no fierce
sunlight.
Care: water liberally during growing
period, do not allow compost to dry
out, spray, not too much fertiliser;
drier in winter.
Humidity: high (moisture 'island').
Temperature: 18–20°C in winter.
Repotting: every spring.
Compost: plenty of loamy humus,
leafmould; or pre-packed potting
compost.
Propagation: stem-tip or stem
section cuttings, preferably
containing an 'eye' root.

Pittosporum
Australian Laurel, Mock Orange,
Japanese Pittosporum or Victorian
Box

Flowering: spring, summer.
Situation: good light.
Care: water freely with lime-free
water and feed when growing,
preferably with organic fertiliser
(lime-free); water as required in
winter.
Humidity: moderate.
Temperature: 4–8°C in winter.
Repotting: in spring, if necessary.
Compost: potting compost; loam,
rotted cow manure and peat fibre;
or pre-packed garden peat mix.
Propagation: cuttings, from seed.

Platycerium
Stag-horn Fern or Elkhorn

Flowering: none—ferns do not
flower.
Situation: moderate light.
Care: do not spray or sponge leaves;
as hanging plant immerse in tepid
water twice a week; as standing-
plant water normally.
Humidity: fairly high.
Temperature: 18–22°C.
Repotting: not often; in spring.
Compost: leafmould, garden peat,
rotted cow manure, sphagnum moss;
if grown on cork-bark, wrap a ball
of leafmould or compost around
roots and secure with soft wire.
Propagation: by division, from seed.

Plectranthus
Swedish Ivy, Candle Plant or
Rheumatism Plant

Flowering: summer and autumn.
Situation: light, no direct sunlight.
Care: water fairly freely when
growing, immerse in water twice a
week and feed; keep cooler and drier
after flowering; do not feed in winter.
Humidity: preferably high.
Temperature: 18–20°C; not below
12°C in winter.
Repotting: in spring, if necessary.
Compost: leafmould, rotted cow
manure, sharp sand; or proprietary
loam-based compost.
Propagation: cuttings (stem-tip) in
spring, from seed.

Pleione

Flowering: April–May.
Situation: moderate light, fresh air,
cool.
Care: spray daily during growing
period, keep drier after flowering and
dry off completely when leaves turn
yellow.
Humidity: high.
Temperature: approx. 12C°; not
below 4°C in winter.
Repotting: every three years—after
flowering.
Compost: osmunda fibre, peat,
sphagnum moss.
Propagation: pseudo-bulbs (offsets),
from seed.

Plumbago
Cape Leadwort

Flowering: spring–autumn.
Situation: good light, no fierce sunlight.
Care: water freely, feed every fortnight; keep drier and cooler in winter, do not feed.
Humidity: high (water 'island').
Temperature: above 15°C; not under 4°C in the winter.
Repotting: October, when necessary.
Compost: leafmould, rotted cow manure, sharp sand; or proprietary loam-based compost.
Propagation: stem-tip cuttings from pruned back plants.

Polyscias

Flowering: seldom in cultivation.
Situation: warm and shady, out of direct sun.
Care: spray frequently and water with lime-free water, feed every two weeks; keep drier in winter and withhold feed.
Humidity: high throughout the year.
Temperature: not under 16°C in winter.
Repotting: in spring, if necessary.
Compost: potting compost, clay, sharp sand.
Propagation: cuttings, from seed.

Polystichum
Shield Fern or Christmas Fern

Flowering: none—ferns do not flower.
Situation: moderate light, no sunlight; can go outdoors in summer.
Care: water freely, spray occasionally, feed every 2–3 weeks; water more sparingly in winter and do not feed.
Humidity: high (surround with moist air—'island').
Temperature: cool; 6–10°C in winter.
Repotting: every two years; in spring.
Compost: leafmould, sharp sand, rotted cow manure; or proprietary loam-based compost or peat mix.
Propagation: remove offset bulbs with leaf, sowing of spores.

Primula
Primrose

Flowering: winter and spring.
Situation: moderate light, no sunlight.
Care: plenty of fresh air, not too much (lime-free) water, feed weekly; remove old flowers; *P. obconica* can irritate skin allergies.
Humidity: moderate.
Temperature: 10–15°C; winter minimum of 10°C.
Repotting: perennial; only when essential.
Compost: potting compost, peat, sharp sand (no leafmould).
Propagation: from seed.

Pseuderanthemum

Flowering: summer.
Situation: good light without direct sunlight, warm.
Care: water when soil feels dry and feed every 3 weeks; keep drier in winter, withhold feed; use lime-free water.
Humidity: high.
Temperature: not falling below 16°C in winter, preferably 18–20°C.
Repotting: spring (shallow pot).
Compost: proprietary loam-based compost.
Propagation: cuttings.

Pteris
Brake, Ribbon Fern, Sword Brake or Variegated Table Fern

Flowering: none—ferns do not flower.
Situation: moderate light, no sun.
Care: water liberally with soft (lime-free) water, feed every 14 days, spray regularly; water more sparingly in winter and withhold feed.
Humidity: high ('island').
Temperature: moderately warm; not below 10–12°C in winter.
Repotting: not often; spring.
Compost: woodland soil or leafmould, peat fibre, rotted cow manure; or proprietary peat compost.
Propagation: by division, from seed.

Punica
Pomegranate

Flowering: summer, then fruits.
Situation: sunny and warm in summer, can go outdoors then; cool in winter.
Care: plenty of fresh air; gradually increase watering when new shoots appear and feed weekly; water only sparingly after flowering and withhold feed in the winter.
Humidity: fairly low.
Temperature: 5°C in winter.
Repotting: rarely necessary.
Compost: leafmould, loam, sharp sand; or ready-mixed loam-based compost.
Propagation: from cuttings in the spring.

Rebutia
Mexican Sunball

Flowering: spring and early summer.
Situation: summer: warm and sunny; winter: light and cool.
Care: keep dry in winter; water normally when buds develop, do not allow to dry out and do not turn the pot; feed from April to July with special cactus fertiliser.
Humidity: high in summer.
Temperature: approx. 7°C in winter.
Repotting: rarely necessary.
Compost: sandy leafmould or special cactus compost.
Propagation: cuttings; from seed.

Rechsteineria
Cardinal Flower

Flowering: summer, autumn.
Situation: good light, out of sunlight, warm.
Care: water fairly freely but not on the tuber or foliage; do not spray; feed fortnightly; keep tubers dry in their pots in winter.
Humidity: high.
Temperature: approx. 12°C in winter.
Repotting: plant tubers in fresh compost in Feb–March.
Compost: leafmould, peat, rotted cow manure; or proprietary peat mix.
Propagation: cuttings; from seed.

Rhaphidophora aures (Scindapsus aureus)
Devil's Ivy

Flowering: none.
Situation: good light, no sunlight, warm.
Care: water when soil feels dry, sponge leaves, spray occasionally, feed every month throughout the year; keep drier in winter.
Humidity: fairly high.
Temperature: not below 12°C in winter.
Repotting: when necessary.
Compost: proprietary loam-based compost or peat mix.
Propagation: cuttings (in water), also stem sections.

Rhipsalidopsis
Easter Cactus

Flowering: spring.
Situation: semi-shade, no direct sun.
Care: water freely during growing period with lime-free water, syringe leaves; once a month cactus fertiliser; gradually reduce watering after flowering, then more freely as new buds form; do not turn pot.
Humidity: high (good air moisture).
Temperature: 10–12°C in winter; 15–18°C after bud development.
Repotting: when necessary, after flowering.
Compost: leafmould, sharp sand and peat fibre.
Propagation: cuttings.

Rhipsalis
Mistletoe Cactus or
Snowdrop Cactus

Flowering: autumn and winter.
Situation: semi-shade, no sunlight.
Care: water freely and feed every 14 days in the summer; drier and cooler before and after flowering and no fertiliser.
Humidity: preferably high.
Temperature: warm, resting period (autumn) fairly cool.
Repotting: after flowering, when necessary.
Compost: leafmould, garden soil, peat, sharp sand; or special cactus soil.
Propagation: cuttings, from seed.

Rhododendron indicum, syn. Azalea indica
Japanese Azalea, Azalea

Flowering: autumn, winter, spring.
Situation: screen from direct sunlight, light, fairly cool, provide plenty of fresh air.
Care: water freely, spray buds with tepid, lime-free water; immerse plant occasionally, feed with lime-free fertiliser.
Humidity: high.
Temperature: 19°C maximum, when in full flower.
Repotting: rarely necessary; in spring.
Compost: lime-free humusy soil; or special azalea compost.
Propagation: cuttings, from seed.

Rhoeo
Moses-in-the-Cradle or Boat Lily

Flowering: May–June (insignificant).
Situation: semi-shade, good light in winter, no sunlight.
Care: water freely from March to August, spray regularly, feed once a week, then gradually reduce watering and withhold feed.
Humidity: high.
Temperature: 16–20°C.
Repotting: in spring.
Compost: peat-based potting compost, sharp sand.
Propagation: side-shoot cuttings, from seed.

Rhoicissus rhomboidea, syn. Cissus rhombifolia
Grape Ivy or Natal Vine

Flowering: only mature plants.
Situation: semi-shade, no direct sunlight.
Care: keep soil moist but not wet, feed each month throughout the year; spray.
Humidity: high.
Temperature: cool or moderately warm, 16–20°C; minimum in winter of 12°C.
Compost: garden peat-based potting compost with a little rotted cow manure or humus.
Propagation: lateral shoot cuttings.

Rivina

Flowering: spring–summer, berries.
Situation: plenty of light, no strong summer sunlight.
Care: keep moderately moist, feed once every 3 weeks; prune back after the berries have fallen.
Humidity: moderate.
Temperature: also moderate; minimum of 13°C.
Repotting: in the spring.
Compost: leafmould, sharp sand; or proprietary loam-based compost.
Propagation: by division, cuttings.

Rochea coccinea

Flowering: summer.
Situation: good light, no strong sunlight in summer; sheltered in the garden.
Care: guard against overwatering—only water when soil feels dry; feed every 14 days in the growing season; keep drier and do not feed in winter.
Humidity: moderate.
Temperature: 8–10°C in winter.
Repotting: rarely necessary; after flowering.
Compost: leafmould, clay, sharp sand; or proprietary loam-based compost.
Propagation: cuttings, from seed.

Rosa
Rose

Flowering: summer.
Situation: light, sunny, plenty of fresh air; preferably outdoors in summer.
Care: keep well moist during growing and flowering season, feed twice a week; remove dead flowers; keep cool and drier in winter and withhold feed.
Humidity: high.
Temperature: around 7°C in winter.
Repotting: spring, when pruning.
Compost: leafmould, clay, rotted cow manure.
Propagation: from seed.

Saintpaulia
African Violet

Flowering: more than once a year.
Situation: semi-shade, out of strong sunlight.
Care: water normally, preferably with lime-free water on the drainage saucer; feed every 14 days during flowering period; keep drier after flowering.
Humidity: high ('island' in water).
Temperature: 16–22°C; minimum of 16°C.
Repotting: rarely necessary (shallow pot).
Compost: peat-based potting compost with some rotted cow manure.
Propagation: cuttings, from seed.

Sanchezia

Flowering: autumn (late) and winter.
Situation: good light, out of sunlight.
Care: keep soil moist, spray regularly and sponge leaves; feed every 14 days; withhold feed after flowering, but provide warmth and light.
Humidity: high (set on 'island' in water).
Temperature: 18–25°C (throughout the year).
Repotting: in spring, if necessary.
Compost: proprietary loam-based potting compost with some sharp sand and rotted cow manure.
Propagation: cuttings (in water) or in peat fibre and sharp sand mix.

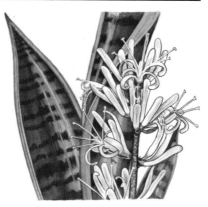

Sansevieria
Mother-in-Law's Tongue, Bow String Hemp or Snake Plant

Flowering: not often; generally in the spring or early summer (insignificant flower clusters).
Situation: plenty of light, sunny.
Care: water regularly (fairly warm) and feed every 14 days in summer; keep drier and do not feed in winter.
Humidity: low.
Temperature: not below 15°C in winter.
Repotting: when plant pushes up out of the pot.
Compost: proprietary loam-based compost or peat mix.
Propagation: by division, leaf cuttings.

Sauromatum
Monarch of the East

Flowering: early spring.
Situation: good light, can go outdoors in summer but bring inside in November.
Care: bring into flower without any soil or water (smells like a Carrion Flower!), then pot up; water and feed.
Humidity: low.
Temperature: 6–8°C in winter.
Repotting: after flowering (large pot).
Compost: leafmould or garden soil with some rotted cow manure.
Propagation: from offsets, which will flower after 2–3 years.

Saxifraga
Mother of Thousands, Aaron's Beard, Strawberry Geranium or Strawberry Begonia

Flowering: early summer.
Situation: good light in half-shady location, no direct sunlight.
Care: keep moderately moist and feed fortnightly during growing season; drier and cooler between Oct–Feb, no feed.
Humidity: fairly high.
Temperature: normal room temperature; min. of 8°C in winter; variegated cultivar better at 15°C.
Repotting: in spring—shallow pot.
Compost: leafmould, peat, sand.
Propagation: pot up plantlets.

Schefflera
Umbrella Tree

Flowering: does not normally flower.
Situation: good light, no direct sunlight, plenty of fresh air; can go outdoors in summer.
Care: water generously in the growing season, feed once a week, spray, and possibly treat with leaf-gloss every three weeks; keep cooler and drier from October onwards.
Humidity: moderate.
Temperature: preferably 12–17°C.
Repotting: rarely; in the spring.
Compost: proprietary loam-based compost.
Propagation: from seeds sown in spring.

Scilla
Squill

Flowering: primarily in the spring.
Situation: light and sunny when flowering; pot up in dark, cool location.
Care: do not allow compost to dry out; move to light, warm spot when shoots are approx. 5cms long.
Humidity: moderate.
Temperature: 10–20°C when flowering.
Repotting: October–November set bulbs in dish.
Compost: proprietary loam-based compost.
Propagation: by removal of offsets from the bulbs in autumn, from seed. Plant bulbs in garden after flowering.

Scindapsus pictus
Ivy Arum or Devil's Ivy

Flowering: none.
Situation: very good light but out of direct sunlight.
Care: keep soil moist with tepid water, spray occasionally in summer, feed monthly, sponge leaves.
Humidity: moderate.
Temperature: 16–20°C; min. winter of 12°C.
Repotting: when necessary.
Compost: leafmould, rotted cow manure, sharp sand; or proprietary peat compost.
Propagation: cuttings (in water) in dark location.

Scirpus
Miniature Bulrush or Club Rush

Flowering: summer.
Situation: semi-shade, no direct sunlight.
Care: water freely on the drainage dish during growing period; moderately warm location.
Humidity: very high (provide air moisture).
Temperature: 10–15°C.
Repotting: spring, if necessary.
Compost: proprietary potting compost with a little clay or loam.
Propagation: by division, from seed.

Sedum
Stonecrop

Flowering: according to the species.
Situation: good light, some sunlight.
Care: water when soil feels dry; it is not advisable to feed; keep almost dry and cool in winter.
Humidity: low.
Temperature: 8–10°C in winter.
Repotting: rarely necessary (slightly larger, shallow pot).
Compost: leafmould, sharp sand.
Propagation: cuttings, from seed, by division.

Selaginella
Creeping Moss, Moss Fern or Spike Moss

Flowering: none.
Situation: light, no sunlight, warm.
Care: plenty of rainwater, spray frequently; compost must not dry out; feed every 14 days.
Humidity: fairly high.
Temperature: 15°C minimum in winter.
Repotting: when necessary.
Compost: proprietary peat-based compost.
Propagation: cuttings (5cms long), by division.

Selenicereus
Queen of the Night or Night Cactus

Flowering: summer.
Situation: moderate sunlight, warm, moist.
Care: water liberally in the summer, sparingly in winter; spray until plant flowers; feed with cactus fertiliser in the summer.
Humidity: high.
Temperature: min. of 10°C in winter.
Repotting: plastic pot, small plants in spring, mature plants when necessary.
Compost: pre-packed potting compost, sharp sand; or special cactus soil.
Propagation: cuttings, from seed.

Senecio
Cinereria, Candle Plant, String of
Beads or California Geranium

Flowering: according to the species.
Situation: light or semi-shade, not
sunny, warm in summer, cool in
winter.
Care: water moderately when
growing, feed every other month;
keep fairly dry in winter.
Humidity: low.
Temperature: min. of 8°C in winter.
Repotting: only when necessary
(shallow pot).
Compost: leafmould, sharp sand,
fine clay; or pre-packed potting
compost.
Propagation: cuttings, runners.

Setcreasea
Purple Heart

Flowering: summer.
Situation: plenty of light, sunlight, in
order to maintain the purple leaf
colour.
Care: keep nice and moist but not
wet during growing period; feed
occasionally; water more sparingly
from autumn onwards.
Humidity: fairly high.
Temperature: 16–20°C.
Repotting: March–April.
Compost: leafmould, fine clay, rotted
cow manure; or loam-based compost
or proprietary peat mix.
Propagation: cuttings.

Siderasis

Flowering: summer.
Situation: semi-shade, damp and
warm.
Care: keep compost moist but not
wet, feed every 14 days; provide
humid atmosphere.
Humidity: high ('island').
Temperature: not below 16°C in
winter; 18–22°C during the day.
Repotting: spring (shallow pot).
Compost: pre-packed potting
compost.
Propagation: only by division.

Sinningia
Gloxinia or Cinderella Slippers

Flowering: spring–summer.
Situation: good light, out of direct
sunlight.
Care: water when compost feels dry;
spray until buds appear, feed every
fortnight; keep drier and do not
feed after flowering.
Humidity: high (set on 'island' in
water or moist peat).
Temperature: 20°C; winter min. 6°C.
Repotting: pot up tubers in
February–March.
Compost: proprietary peat compost.
Propagation: cuttings, runners with
attached shoots.

Smithiantha
Temple Bells

Flowering: summer–autumn.
Situation: plenty of light, no direct
sunlight.
Care: keep soil moderately moist
with tepid water; syringe leaves
(overhead) a few times a day; keep
drier as foliage dies off.
Humidity: high ('island').
Temperature: 21°C; winter 10–12°C.
Repotting: spring—repot rhizomes in
fresh compost.
Compost: pre-packed garden peat-
based compost; peat, rotted cow
manure.
Propagation: by division of rhizome,
by leaf cuttings.

Solanum capsicastrum
Winter Cherry or Christmas Cherry

Flowering: summer, followed by
berries.
Situation: outdoors in summer,
sunny location; winter: light.
Care: keep well moistened, spray
now and then over the berries; prune
back to above the berries in spring
and autumn.
Humidity: high (water 'island').
Temperature: 8–10°C in winter.
Repotting: spring (slightly larger pot).
Compost: potting compost with
rotted cow manure and some loam.
Propagation: from seed.

Soleirolia
Baby's Tears, Mind-your-own-business or Angel's Tears

Flowering: insignificant; greenish flowering habit.
Situation: moderately light to shady.
Care: water moderately, feed once a month during growing season.
Humidity: fairly high.
Temperature: from 12°C; maximum of 18°C.
Repotting: spring, if necessary.
Compost: pre-packed loam-based compost.
Propagation: by division.

Sonerila
Frosted Sonerila

Flowering: autumn, and variously.
Situation: warm, moist and shady.
Care: provide plant with warm, humid atmosphere, water freely on soil with lukewarm water; do not spray foliage; feed every 14 days in spring and summer.
Humidity: high.
Temperature: above 20°C.
Repotting: infrequently; only when roots grow through drainage hole.
Compost: leafmould, sphagnum moss and sharp sand; or proprietary peat compost.
Propagation: cuttings, from seed.

Sparmannia
African Hemp, House Lime or African Linden

Flowering: winter–spring.
Situation: good light, no strong sunlight, fresh air, fairly cool.
Care: water moderately during growing and flowering season, more in summer, sparingly in the resting period (May–July); feed every 14 days but not after flowering.
Humidity: not too low.
Temperature: 5–10°C in winter.
Repotting: after the resting period (July).
Compost: leafmould and garden compost, rotted cow manure; or proprietary loam-based compost.
Propagation: cuttings (after pruning).

Spathiphyllum
Lily of Peace

Flowering: summer.
Situation: semi- to deep-shade.
Care: keep evenly moist, feed every 14 days when growing and flowering, spray occasionally.
Humidity: high.
Temperature: minimum of 16°C in winter.
Repotting: Feb–March (not too large a pot).
Compost: proprietary peat mix or loam-based compost; or fine clay or loam, some rotted cow manure.
Propagation: by division or from seed.

Stapelia
Carrion Flower

Flowering: summer.
Situation: warm, no strong sunlight.
Care: guard against saturated soil (good drainage), keep cool, dryish and place in good light in winter.
Humidity: low.
Temperature: around 10°C in winter.
Repotting: rarely (shallow pot).
Compost: plenty of clay or loam, some sharp sand, chalk gravel (no leafmould, garden compost is better).
Propagation: cuttings; from seed.

Stephanotis
Madagascar Jasmine or Clustered Wax Flower

Flowering: summer–autumn.
Situation: good light, out of strong sunlight.
Care: water freely when growing and flowering, spray daily, feed every 14 days; keep fairly dry in winter, but continue to spray.
Humidity: high (on 'island' in water).
Temperature: 12–18°C; winter min. 12°C.
Repotting: young plants in the spring.
Compost: proprietary loam-based compost, or peat mix.
Propagation: cuttings, possibly from seed.

Strelitzia
Bird of Paradise Flower or
Crane Plant

Flowering: spring–summer.
Situation: light, no strong sunlight.
Care: plenty of fresh air in summer;
rest from May to Aug, water sparingly,
gradually increase, spray, feed
weekly; keep drier in winter.
Humidity: moderate.
Temperature: 18–20°C; winter 10°C.
Repotting: rarely (roomy pot).
Compost: proprietary loam-based
compost.
Propagation: by division or from
seed.

Streptocarpus
Cape Primrose

Flowering: summer (prolonged).
Situation: good light, no strong
sunlight.
Care: water freely with tepid water
on the saucer; it is better not to feed;
keep drier after flowering; dry and
cool in winter.
Humidity: high ('island').
Temperature: approx: 18°C; winter
min. of 6°C.
Repotting: Feb–March, every year.
Compost: leafmould, peat, rotted cow
manure; or proprietary garden peat
mix with extra fertiliser.
Propagation: leaf cuttings, from seed.

Syngonium
Goosefoot Plant or Arrowhead
Plant

Flowering: seldom in cultivation.
Situation: well-shaded, warm.
Care: keep soil evenly moist, sponge
leaves, spray frequently, feed every
14 days, not in winter.
Humidity: high ('island').
Temperature: 15–22°C.
Repotting: only when pot is too small.
Compost: leafmould, sharp sand,
peat; or potting compost with sharp
sand and peat.
Propagation: stem-tip cuttings.

Tetrastigma
Chestnut Vine or Lizard Plant

Flowering: not in cultivation.
Situation: lots of light, no sunlight,
fresh air, warm.
Care: water freely in summer and
feed monthly; keep drier in spring
and autumn, drier still in winter;
spray throughout the year.
Humidity: moderate.
Temperature: 12°C min. in winter.
Repotting: spring (roomy pot).
Compost: loam-based compost or
proprietary peat mix.
Propagation: cuttings and stem
sections with leaf.

Thunbergia
Black-eyed Susan or
Black-eyed Clockvine

Flowering: early summer–autumn.
Situation: good light, sunny, no
strong noonday sunlight.
Care: water freely and feed weekly
when growing, ventilate well; keep
drier in winter; cut back rigorously
in February.
Humidity: not too low.
Temperature: 18–20°C; winter 10°C.
Repotting: difficult to keep over.
Compost: leafmould, sharp sand,
lime; or proprietary loam-based
compost.
Propagation: from seed.

Tillandsia
Blue Flowered Torch or
Spanish Moss

Flowering: according to the species.
Situation: good light, no strong
sunlight.
Care: spray regularly with lukewarm
water; feed weekly; water
moderately in winter.
Humidity: high.
Temperature: normally heated room;
winter min. 13°C.
Repotting: when shoots reach half
the length of parent plant.
Compost: chopped sphagnum moss,
beechleaf soil, rotted cow manure.
Propagation: by division.

139

Tolmiea
Piggyback Plant or Mother of Thousands

Flowering: spring (insignificant).
Situation: light, no strong sunlight.
Care: water moderately in the growing period, feed every 14 days, ventilate well; keep drier and cooler in winter.
Humidity: high or moderate.
Temperature: 10°C minimum in winter.
Repotting: spring; rarely necessary.
Compost: potting compost, sharp sand, rotted cow manure.
Propagation: from baby plantlets.

Torenia
Wishbone Flower

Flowering: June–September.
Situation: light, sunshine (screen lightly in summer).
Care: water fairly freely, feed every 14 days, ventilate well; discard in the winter.
Humidity: moderate.
Temperature: not below 10°C.
Repotting: annual plant.
Compost: pre-packed potting compost, sharp sand.
Propagation: from seed in Feb–March.

Tradescantia
Wandering Jew, Spiderwort or Inch Plant

Flowering: summer.
Situation: well lit, little sun.
Care: water when the soil feels dry; feed fortnightly from March; keep drier and withhold feed in winter; take cuttings annually.
Humidity: moderate.
Temperature: cool; winter min. of 10°C.
Repotting: when pot is root-bound.
Compost: pre-packed potting compost, rotted cow manure, sharp sand.
Propagation: from cuttings, by division.

Vallota
Scarborough Lily

Flowering: summer–autumn.
Situation: plenty of light, screen from strong sunlight.
Care: provide more warmth and water from Feb onwards, feed during growing and flowering period; keep cool after flowering.
Humidity: moderate.
Temperature: 18–20°C; in winter 8°C.
Repotting: every 2–3 years in Feb–March; neck of bulb above soil.
Compost: potting compost, sharp sand, peat, rotted cow manure.
Propagation: from offsets when potting.

Vanda

Flowering: according to the species.
Situation: plenty of light, sunny.
Care: water generously in summer with soft water; keep drier in winter; spray only when weather is hot; feed every 14 days in summer (lime-free).
Humidity: high.
Temperature: 20–30°C; 12–18°C in winter, never below 12°C.
Repotting: spring, if necessary.
Compost: osmunda fibre, sphagnum moss, crocks.
Propagation: by division and from seed.

Veltheimia
Forest Lily

Flowering: February–April.
Situation: plenty of light, cool.
Care: water liberally during growth and flowering, feed occasionally; drier in resting period May–Sept.
Humidity: moderately moist.
Temperature: 10–12°C during the day.
Repotting: pot up bulb in Sept.
Compost: potting compost, rotted cow manure, some clay (half cover bulb).
Propagation: bulb offsets, from seed.

Vitis

Flowering: spring, followed by berries.
Situation: full sunlight, moderately warm.
Care: water freely in summer, spray regularly, feed every 14 days; keep drier and do not feed from December on.
Humidity: not too low.
Temperature: minimum of 15°C.
Repotting: spring (also prune back).
Compost: garden soil, leafmould; or potting compost with rotted cow manure and peat.
Propagation: cuttings (in water or rooting compost).

Vriesea
Flaming Sword

Flowering: but once, in the spring.
Situation: good light, no strong sunlight.
Care: constant warmth, soil moderately moist, spray regularly; water in the leaf funnel in summer; feed fortnightly.
Humidity: high.
Temperature: 18–20°C in winter.
Repotting: plant develops offsets.
Compost: leafmould, sphagnum moss, osmunda fibre, rotted cow manure; or special bromeliad compost.
Propagation: from rooted offsets at half the height of mother plant.

Yucca
Palm Lily

Flowering: summer (mature specimens); flowers best outdoors.
Situation: light, warm in summer; can go outdoors; cool in winter.
Care: water fairly freely in summer, feed weekly; keep drier in winter and withhold feed.
Humidity: moderate to low.
Temperature: around 6°C in winter.
Repotting: spring.
Compost: loam, sharp sand; or proprietary loam-based compost.
Propagation: by division, from seed.

Zantedeschia
Arum Lily, Calla Lily or Lily of the Nile

Flowering: winter–spring.
Situation: cool during winter-flowering; in garden July–Sept., light.
Care: feed weekly and water freely during growing and flowering period, spray; rest in May–June, then very little water and no fertiliser.
Humidity: high when flowering.
Temperature: cool; winter max. 14°C, min. 8°C.
Repotting: June–July.
Compost: garden soil, leafmould; or proprietary peat mix.
Propagation: divide rootstock.

Zebrina
Wandering Jew or Bronze Inch Plant

Flowering: summer–autumn.
Situation: moderately light; variegated species more light, no strong sunlight.
Care: keep evenly moist; feed fortnightly March–Sept; keep drier in winter.
Humidity: moderate.
Temperature: 15°C minimum in winter.
Repotting: when necessary, if pot is root-bound.
Compost: potting compost, sharp sand.
Propagation: by division, or from cuttings.

Zygocactus
Christmas Cactus or Lobster Cactus

Flowering: winter.
Situation: good light, no direct sunlight, cool.
Care: do not turn pot during bud development or flowering; water freely and feed every 14 days; keep cooler and drier in Sept to bud development and withhold feed.
Humidity: high.
Temperature: when in bud 16–18°C.
Repotting: spring, if necessary.
Compost: leafmould, garden compost, sharp sand, fine clay and peat fibre; or proprietary loam- or peat-based compost, humusy and rich.
Propagation: cuttings of stem-leaves.

141

Index

Picture credits

l = left, r = right, a = above,
b = below, c = centre

ABC-press IMS-interieur 79
Johannes Apel 16lb
Ardea Photographics 20lb
R. Becking 31lb
Centraal Beheer 8lc
Jan van Dommelen 30rb
H. Glas 38la
Kees Hageman 68-69 70l 70r 71la 71lb
  72lc 73 74b 76l 77 78lb 80l 80r 81b
  84lb 85l 85ra 86r 87l 87ra 88 89lb 90
  91ra 92la 92lb 93 94-95 96 97la 98ra
  98rb 99 100a
Jan den Hengst 65 66rb 67 72la 72lb
  72r 82l 82rb 83 84r 85rb 86l 87rb
  89a 89rb 91l 92ra 98lb 98lb 100lb
  100rb 101

Rob Herwig 10lb 10r 11la 11lb 11ra
  11rb 16r 18lb 22lc 22cb 25lb 30cb
  30rb 31la 39lb
Henk van der Heyden 84la
Theo Heymans 13rb 17rb 24 25la
  36b 37ra 37rc
Christiane Hilaire 17ra 27lb
Peter ten Hoopen 9
Dr Hans Jesse 13l 16la 19ra 21b 29ra
H. Koster 13ra
Foto Lans 29rb 38r
Lavinia Press 18la 19l
B. Lotgering 31ra
A. van den Nieuwenhuizen 8r 21a
  34rb 35
Rob de Nooy 9lrb
Fotoarchiv Paris Match/Marie-Claire
  66la 71r 97r
Studio Van Passel 32b
Hannes Rosenberg 19rb 32a

W. Schacht 25r
Heinz Schrempp 23 34l 34rb 39lc
Fotoarchief Scoop (Bouillard) 82lb
Frans Siebeling 22rb 40a 40c
Pim Smit 75la 81b
Fotoarchief Spaarnestad 14b 26la 26lb
  27cb 27ra 27rc 27rb 32c 33 36a;
  foto's Harry Pot 75lb 75r 76r
Fotoarchief Het Spectrum bv 22lb
Wolfram Stehling 18r 19rc 26r 39la 40b
Jan Sterk 6
Liselotte Straub 12 15 17l 20rb 28c
  29rc 30ra 31rb 38lb
Syndication International 8la 8lb
  10la 14a 14c 17rc 28a 29l 31rb
Julia Voskuil 39ra
Fotoarchief VT-wonen 74a 78cb 97lb
Gebr Ypma bv 37b
**Black and white illustrations, Meir
  Salomon, Studio** 78

Illustrations in alphabetical section
Ko van den Broecke, Louis Chartrer,
Kees van Daal, J. van Dam,
P. Gofferjé, Gabrielle Gossner,
Christiane Hilaire, Richard Hook,
Kees de Kiefte, Marius Kolvoort,
Kothuis Art-team, Erik Meeder,
Harry Mesker, Sylvie Monti, Erno
Tromp, Jos van Uytregt

The publishers are grateful to Seale-
Hayne College, Newton Abbot, for
their botanical assistance.